12/2018 –

Becoming Myself
A Journey of Healing and Transformation

EILEEN TURNER

Copyright © 2018 Eileen Turner.

All rights reserved. No part of this book may be reproduced, stored, or transmitted by any means—whether auditory, graphic, mechanical, or electronic—without written permission of the author, except in the case of brief excerpts used in critical articles and reviews. Unauthorized reproduction of any part of this work is illegal and is punishable by law.

Scripture quotations are from New Revised Standard Version Bible, copyright © 1989 National Council of the Churches of Christ in the United States of America. Used by permission. All rights reserved worldwide.

This book is a work of non-fiction. Unless otherwise noted, the author and the publisher make no explicit guarantees as to the accuracy of the information contained in this book and in some cases, names of people and places have been altered to protect their privacy.

ISBN: 978-1-4834-9299-5 (sc)
ISBN: 978-1-4834-9298-8 (e)

Because of the dynamic nature of the Internet, any web addresses or links contained in this book may have changed since publication and may no longer be valid. The views expressed in this work are solely those of the author and do not necessarily reflect the views of the publisher, and the publisher hereby disclaims any responsibility for them.

Any people depicted in stock imagery provided by Getty Images are models, and such images are being used for illustrative purposes only. Certain stock imagery © Getty Images.

Lulu Publishing Services rev. date: 11/30/2018

Prologue

A few weeks into retirement, propelled by a notion that I would have the best kind of future after I made some sense of the past, I began writing an autobiography. Many incidents lay unexamined and seemed fragmented and disjointed. There were so many times of upheaval and loss—and incredible moments of joy. I hoped that writing might reveal connections between the various pieces, and that perhaps some pattern would emerge.

I intentionally decided to examine the past from a faith perspective, especially when examining painful memories. I wanted to see the good I could not see when I was living it, surviving it, moving on. I wanted to allow time for conclusions other than judgement (toward both myself and others) to emerge. The work was slow, invigorating and exhausting. Surprises kept happening. Compassion kept growing.

I wrote twelve chapters. Each chronicled a particular place, community or relationship that formed or changed me. I struggled over whether to write the chapter I titled *She Needs Me*. What happened was too personal, too shameful, too bizarre. Yet, to give a full account of my life, in it went. Not only was it part of my life, it is what changed me the most. It is the Before and After of who I am. It is where this memoir begins.

To protect the confidential nature of our relationship and the right for privacy, names and locations have been changed. I have not knowingly altered any of the events.

Chapter One

Standing in front of my dresser, a hurriedly packed suitcase on the floor beside me, I pause and take a breath. *God, is this really your will for me? To leave Matthew and Andrew?* I wait for some small sign, a feeling, an uneasiness that might prompt me to stay. All I feel is a sense of calm. *They'll me alright without me. They have their dad.*

I turn around, glance at the pile of laundered socks on the bed that need to be sorted, pick up the suitcase, walk out of the house, open the car door, turn to Sarah and say "Let's go."

Why did I take such a drastic measure? What drove me to walk out of my life, to desert my eleven and nine year-old sons? Three decades have passed, and I must now try to recount who I was back then. To begin, I go back eight years.

We were a small group of religious seekers, mostly young mothers, who met at our Lutheran church every Tuesday morning for Bible study and prayer. Pat, a gregarious woman who often brought comic relief, heard about a gifted Bible teacher and suggested we invite her to our group for a few weeks. We liked her so much she stayed for three years.

Beverly was a petite, soft-spoken, amiable stay-at-home mother in her early forties with no college education or formal theological training. The tepid atmosphere most of us felt in our church sharply contrasted to the passion emanating from Beverly. We were intrigued with how Jesus came to be so real for her. He was her best friend. She loved him, sang songs to him, wanted to be like him, wept when depicting the physical torment and abandonment Jesus experienced on the cross.

Beverly had been forced to leave her church after she refused to stop teaching about a baptism of the Holy Spirit, an event contrary to Baptist doctrine. Leaving church and friends so central to her life had been devastating. Yet, like Jesus, she had resolved to follow God's will, even when this led to suffering and sacrifice. Hearing her story endeared her to us even more. To many of us, she became the model of an authentic, faithful Christian.

As Lutherans we believed scripture was the authoritative Word of God. In worship services we heard sermons, sang liturgy and said prayers that were biblically based. But no one had ever taught us the Bible. Everything Beverly taught came straight from its pages and therefore could not be disputed.

Beverly taught us about a supernatural, spiritual realm, distinctly separate from the earthly one. A realm where God ruled, where Jesus had put to death the power and guilt of sin, where the spirit — not sinful flesh or the evil world — was in control. Those who were of this world remained lost and blind, unable to discern the things of God because of their darkened minds. We were the enlightened ones, born of the spirit, separate from the world, and because of this should expect to be misunderstood, even persecuted.

One of her teachings centered around water baptism. She presented verse after verse depicting persons being baptized after they came to faith in God—a clear contradiction of Lutheran practice of infant baptism. When our pastor heard about our changing convictions, he told us we could no longer meet in the church.

Some of us dropped out, like the pastor's wife and a woman on the church board. The rest of us continued to meet at Janet's townhouse. Being exiled bound us together even more. Sitting on the floor at Beverly's feet felt like being one of Jesus' first disciples. No longer clouded by church tradition or doctrine, our eyes were open to the fullness of God's truth.

Beverly also taught us about another kind of baptism — the baptism of the Holy Spirit. Available to every Christian, this baptism imbued one with the power to overcome the sinful desires of the flesh and the evil pull of the world. Oh, how I desired to be transported, to grab hold of, this supernatural power.

The opportunity came at a two day Pentecostal gathering six of us attended. With loud singing, raising of hands, clapping and even dancing, worship couldn't have been more different from our Lutheran orderly service.

Knowing what was to come on the second day, I couldn't sleep. When the invitation to receive the baptism of the Holy Spirit was given my hand immediately shot up. Suddenly the top of my head felt warm and the warmth gently flowed down my body. It felt like a kind of dry liquid being poured over me. There was no out-of-control ecstatic feeling or overwhelming sense of being taken over by some powerful force as I had feared. I thanked God for meeting me in such an unassuming and gentle way.

Afterwards, a woman walked over to me and asked if I had spoken in tongues. I said no. She placed her hand on my shoulder and prayed for me to receive it and when nothing happened others came and joined in. Someone coached me to open my mouth, move my tongue, let my voice follow, say anything.

I kept my eyes closed and my mouth shut. I was not going to become a spectacle or loose control by uttering unintelligible sounds in front of these strangers. I had already been bathed in the Holy Spirit and had no need of any further evidence, even if others did.

The little neighborhood band of renegade Lutherans became even closer. To me, being a member brought a deep sense of belonging and of feeling noticed, even special. When Beverly heard I played guitar, she asked me to be the worship leader by playing the praise and worship songs that preceded her teaching. Although I was never transported to the ecstasy others seemed to experience, being a song leader filled a deep need to contribute, to feel valued and important.

Another event also stands out. At a Pentecostal gathering in a large banquet hall filled with tables set for dinner, Beverly invited me, not only to sit at her table, but right beside her. Never had I felt so honored, so special. A woman who had become my mentor and mother figure had singled me out as her favorite.

But, alas, my husband did not regard me so favorably. As a traditional Lutheran Paul saw me as an apostate, persuading others to go astray, especially when my decision to be baptized (or re-baptized as it were) encouraged three others to do the same. For reasons only he knew, Paul came to the baptism, sat in the back pew of the church and became nauseous when he saw his wife being dunked in a large tank of water.

My religious convictions began to affect my work. Determined to offer clients all I could, I included questions about their relationship with God. Most gave a brief account of their church affiliation. Two clients complained to my supervisor. He called me to his office, complimented me on the good work I was doing, reminded me that we were a secular agency and asked me to stop bringing up God. I told him I would not and happily resigned.

I briefly considered tearing up my social work diploma. I no longer needed this worldly knowledge; God and the Bible were enough. Common sense and reason stopped me. Despite this, common sense would not be enough to prevent me from entering the religious delusion that was to come.

Paul began talking about wanting to move back to his home state of Wisconsin, "where the air is cleaner." Everything in me railed against it. I could not imagine leaving a group of women who had become family. Yet I knew what the Bible, ergo God, said: a wife is to submit to her husband. If Paul wanted to go, I must willingly, without resentment, go. In no way was I willing, and angrily told God all the reasons I could not, would not move. Somehow being honest and getting all my objections out opened a window of acceptance and I told Paul I agreed, we should move.

Our townhouse sold quickly and in September of 1979 we drove our station wagon and a moving van from Bowling Green, Ohio to our new home in Eau Claire, Wisconsin just in time for Matthew to begin second grade and Andrew to start first.

Three years later, by all appearances we had adjusted nicely. We had made friends in the Lutheran church just down the street. Paul was teaching middle school history and social studies. Matthew, eleven, and Andrew, nine, were well behaved and popular, excelling in both academics and athletics. I was thirty-eight and held a part-time counselor position in a small, privately funded Christian mental health clinic.

Chapter Two

On a cold, bright January afternoon, Sarah Berkner walked into my office. Casually dressed in muted colors, she was of average height and weight with simply cut brown hair that fell just above her shoulders.

"So what brings you here today, Sarah?" I asked.

"I'm twenty-nine and living with my mother again. It's only temporary but it's still hard. I'm planning on moving into my uncle's house after he moves out."

I nodded, she continued. "I hate living with my mother. She's always interfering in my life, trying to tell me what to do, like I'm a child. When I go into another room she follows me, asking questions about what I'm doing. She can't stand that I have a life apart from her."

"Tell me a little more about your mother," I said.

Sarah described her as a religiously devote woman whose aspirations to be a nun were shattered when she married Sarah's father. Sad most of the time, Sarah tried to make her happy by listening to her pontificate about God and the Catholic Church.

Sarah's destiny was laid out at a very young age. She was to be the nun her mother could not be. Holding this favored position made her two brothers and sister jealous, yet Sarah felt excluded and misunderstand by them.

I was moved as Sarah spoke of her mother's influence, of trying to make her happy, of the role she had been assigned, of feeling misunderstood and excluded. Something about it was familiar, yet I could not put it into words and had no desire to dreg up any of my childhood experiences.

Sarah said her father knew his wife was a "religious fanatic" and went along with it so she wouldn't "crack up." Sarah felt close to her father, especially when he asked her to join him on his errands. Sometimes he was physically abusive toward his three sons, "but this was all in the past." He died shortly after Sarah graduated from high school.

In high school Sarah decided not to pursue a religious vocation, yet without this goal she was left feeling adrift. In college Sarah chose a major in physical therapy because it was the easiest.

Sarah was still struggling with what she wanted to do in life. She saw no future beyond her current job. She added that this had begun in elementary school, when she could not see past the day she would graduate from high school. In fact, she thought that's when she would die.

"I really don't know what it's like to be an adult, making a life of my own. I've tried to be what everybody else wants me to be. Like in high school, I was told all I needed to do was to not completely fail. I knew C's and D's would be good enough because I wasn't talented like my brothers and sisters."

"So since you were never pushed to do more, you never knew what you were really capable of?"

"Yeah. I've always been told I'm lazy. I remember hiding in the closet when us girls were asked to help with the housework. When I was seven I found myself in there and wondered why I was there. Then I knew. Oh yes, I am lazy and I will have to stay here until someone finds me. Sometimes all I want to do is prove to them that they were wrong."

Sarah went on. "They don't understand what I'm going through. It's hard being twenty-nine and single. I have to support myself. All my brothers and sisters are married, except my youngest sister, and now she's engaged."

"Was it hard to accept her engagement?"

"No, I'm happy for her. But I've always felt like an outsider, looking in on others' happiness. Sometimes I think there must be something wrong with me. Why am I still single? Maybe I'm too old to find the good life."

"Twenty-nine's not that old. You have your whole life in front of you." As Sarah fixed her gaze on me I went on. "You know, there are places you could go, things you could do to meet new people." Sarah nodded slightly. We spent some time brainstorming about possibilities.

I asked Sarah about her work.

"For the past two years I've worked in a home for the elderly as a physical therapist. I like my work. People say I'm really sensitive to others needs. I love knitting colorful shawls for residents to put around their shoulders. You know how older people are always cold. Lately they've increased the number of hours I need to put in. It's overwhelming. I'm stressed out. It's too hard."

"Is there any way of negotiating with your supervisor about this, since you're so liked, so respected?

"I've tried that. But it's the institution that lays out the rules. My supervisor sympathizes with me, but she can't do anything."

I asked about places she'd lived before moving in with her mother.

"After college I lived in apartments with roommates, but they all got married or moved somewhere else. I tried living with my older brother and his wife but, you know, it felt like I was a third wheel.

"For the last three years I lived in a charismatic Catholic community. My sister and her husband and three kids were there. It was good. I had my own room, a little refrigerator and hotplate. I ate most of my meals in the dining room with the others."

"So, why did you leave?"

"Well, the leaders always told us to listen to the Lord, but instead, they started telling me what to do. I didn't think their directives (although

Sarah elaborated on these, I cannot now recall them) were the best thing for me. I couldn't trust these leaders anymore. It was really hard to break away from them. I didn't think I was strong enough, but God helped move me out."

During these discussions I drew on what I knew best. I focused on things that could be changed, offered small steps and other directions she could try, reminded her of her strengths, remained optimistic and encouraging. Nothing worked. Sarah had reasons why a suggestion wouldn't work, or she had tried that already. She remained just as stuck as when she first walked into my office. Feeling like a failure, I brought up God.

"Have you turned to God?" I asked. "Prayed? Asked for guidance? strength? Maybe there's some reason you're going through this. Maybe God has a plan in all of it."

"God is always with me. I've known Him all my life." She looked down, then continued. "Even when I was in my mother's womb He was there. When I breathe He's right there. As close as my breath. It's like feeling a mother's arms wrapped around me all the time."

Fascinated, yet skeptical, I thought, *Could any human being have such an early and abiding sense of God?* I probed a little more. "Have there been times you weren't quite sure of God's presence? When you questioned, or doubted, or . . . felt alone?"

"No, I've always felt Him." Sarah looked toward the ceiling and took a breath. "See, when I was a little girl I lived in a perfect place. Like heaven. Everything was so beautiful, peaceful. Full of light. Love was all around me. It was so wonderful. Then, when I was seven, I found myself living on earth. I didn't know how I got there. Everything was different. I cried to God to take me back to where I belonged. But then I guess I just accepted that I had to stay on earth. There was no going back."

I was drawn into Sarah's description of her earliest memories, captivated by her intimate relationship with God, saddened by her jolt into the real world. I had never heard anything like it. To try to make some sense of it I turned to what I'd been taught from the Bible: God's ways are supernatural, far above human understanding. God chooses whomever He wishes, in the way He wishes. Therefore, God must have called Sarah, even before she was born, into a special relationship. Who was I to question this?

After exploring every avenue of help, I concluded there was nothing more I could do and began an exit interview. I told Sarah I had used all the tools in my counseling bag, that I had nothing more to offer. Sarah paused, looked down and said, "Thank you so much for all you've done for me. You've been so kind and understanding. I'll do whatever you say, whatever you think is best."

I was taken aback by this humble act of acceptance and submission, and then felt torn by my decision to end the counseling. It felt like I was abandoning someone who really needed me. I couldn't do that. I told Sarah I would continue seeing her.

Chapter Three

Our sessions suddenly turned in another direction as Sarah began talking about her childhood. She spoke of an older cousin barging in on her while she was sitting on the toilet, of pulling down his pants and asking her to touch it. She thought all the rough hair and that big ugly thing were nasty. She could see it even now.

In another session, Sarah became fidgety and screamed, "Get out of here!" She gagged. "No, no! Choking me. Can't breathe! Can't breathe!" I remained professionally detached yet observant. After a few seconds Sarah caught her breath and opened her eyes. I asked if she was alright, and she said she was fine, that she had known I was in the room the whole time. I was confused. I had heard of trauma being relived in short, hazy snippets, but I hadn't heard of re-enacting an entire childhood trauma so vividly.

In yet another session, Sarah laid on the floor, curled her legs in a fetal position and closed her eyes. "Too tight!" she moaned. "Can't move."

I sat down on the floor beside her, put my hand on her shoulder and asked, "Where are you? What's going on?"

She took a few short breaths, "Something pressing around me. Pushing me down." Panting she yelled, "I don't want to go! Pushing! Down! Can't stop! It hurts! Too bright!" In a few seconds Sarah quieted down and opened her eyes. She sat up. We remained on the floor. I asked if this could have been a birthing experience. She looked down and shrugged her shoulders.

What else could it have been? Yet I had doubts, big doubts. Rationally, I knew that this experience could not have imprinted itself on a fetus's consciousness. But in the end, I put my doubts aside because the experience was felt so vividly by her.

In all of these re-enactments I felt honored that Sarah trusted me enough to talk and act so openly, to allow herself to become so vulnerable. I was proud to have kept my professional composure. But I also knew I was in too deep. My social work degree had not prepared me for this.

"Sarah," I finally said, "I really don't have the necessary training to help you in what you're going through. I think it would be best if you saw someone, maybe a psychologist, with more education around treating childhood trauma."

With a shaky voice she mumbled, "I've already tried that. I can't start over again. I've never been able to open up to anyone like I have with you. I trust you."

How could I pass her on to someone else? Do what everyone else had done? Give up on her? *She is on the path of healing childhood wounds and I am a vital part of this. I can't leave her now.*

When I learned she had seen other professionals I should have asked for their names, sent for their records, spoken to them, gleaned new information and needed perspective. But I did not. Instead, I held onto the conviction that I was better than anyone else. I did not need to hear anything that might cause me to doubt myself or my beliefs.

While standing at the kitchen counter fixing a sandwich for lunch, I considered sharing it with Sarah. I knew that this went outside the bounds of a client/clinician relationship yet thought it could show her that she was accepted and valued, not just as a client, but as a person. And besides, having lunch together would give her more time to decompress. And what would be wrong with that?

As I assembled another sandwich, I decided to wait until after our session, then see if it felt like the right thing to do. It did.

We sat at a table in the commons area. I felt awkward. Sarah, however, seemed quite at ease. I can't recall what we talked about, only that I relished having a conversation where I was not responsible for its direction and no outcome was expected.

After lunch Sarah lit a cigarette and asked if I'd like one. As an ex-smoker (I had quit during my first pregnancy) I smiled and shook my head. A little while later she lit up another, smiled, and teasingly prodded, "You sure you don't want one?" and took a long drag.

I wanted to experience more of this casual, relaxed social time and I thought that there wouldn't be any harm in one, so I accepted her offer. It wasn't long before I became a daily smoker. But worse yet, this was the beginning of a chain of compromises that violated so many professional standards and boundaries that, in the end, I could no longer recognize myself.

As we smoked, Sarah began asking personal questions. I candidly answered. "It must be great to be married!" Sarah exclaimed.

"Marriage isn't all it's made out to be. It's not the be all and end all, you know. Sometimes it's tough. You gotta work at it."

She paused and asked, "What was your maiden name?"

"Eileen Lehto," I repled.

"No, your full name. What was it?"

"Eileen Louise Lehto."

Sarah then began to slowly repeat "Eileen Louise Lehto" over and over again.

It was strange to hear a name I hadn't used for over fifteen years. Then the sound of it became familiar and calming, like a favorite piece of music lost and then found. I felt an opening up — a kind of lightness — as I connected to the person I had been before I married — before my life centered on trying to please my husband, or at least on not upsetting him.

Chapter Four

After Sarah moved into her uncle's house her mental state quickly deteriorated. She obsessed about dangerous things that might happen, felt compelled to write down every thought, took repeated showers without feeling clean, saw herself as dirtier and more lowly than the earth. At times she felt that her hands were disconnected from the rest of her body. She ate very little since feeling full distracted her from thinking. Unable to concentrate at work, she was given a leave of absence.

Sarah also mentioned seeing cat-like shadows slinking across her pillow, rat-like animals running on the floor, little purple snakes on the floor, yet knew they were not real. At times she felt full of rage and envisioned kicking a stranger in the chin, or breaking through a window. Although she said she had never been a drinker, she began to binge drink.

I recommended again that she see the clinic psychiatrist. "He's an older man, real easy to talk to. His office is right around the corner from mine."

"No, I don't want to take any medication. I can get through this. I just need more time."

I should have insisted, but did not. I understood her like on one else. With me by her side, she could be healed. It may look different than any medical, man-made method, but I could trust that the God who had chosen her would continue to show her the way.

Her imagination went to dark places. "I want to cut my stomach open with a sharp knife so I can get out all the bad stuff that's in there. I have to get in deeper. I have to know. To get it out. So I keep probing around with the knife."

"Have you ever acted on this?" I asked.

"No," she replied. "But I can't stop thinking about it." She went on. "Sometimes when I'm driving the car all I can see is that cement embankment. It's right there. All I need to do is turn the wheel. It would be so easy, so fast. If I did it, I know I would go to hell."

"So, what stops you from driving into that wall is knowing you'd go to hell?" I asked. "You really know that would happen?"

"Yeah, I do. The church teaches that suicide is a mortal sin, so I'd never try it."

This was reassuring, but like I'd been taught, I gave her my phone number with a promise she would call me "before doing anything stupid."

A few days later I received a phone call from a social worker at a local hospital. "Are you Sarah Berkner's counselor?"

"Yes I am."

"Sarah called 911 and an ambulance took her to Bethesda Hospital yesterday. She had been drinking heavily and cutting herself, but only superficially. Said she couldn't stop thinking about ways of killing herself. She was admitted to the psychiatric unit and is now resting. Sarah would like to see you. You can come anytime between 9:00am and 7:00pm."

"Okay. I'm so glad she's in a safe place. I'll be there later today. "

"Good, she'll like that."

I hung up, breathed a deep sigh of relief and felt some of the weight I'd been carrying lift off my shoulders. Sarah was finally going to get the help she needed. She was safe. I could stop worrying.

I took my time showering and dressing so I could calm down and not appear rushed or anxious. I needed a veneer of professional composure when I walked onto that unit.

I found the psychiatric wing and introduced myself. The nurse checked Sarah's approved visitor list and said I was the only one on it. She unlocked a heavy mental door and I was led to a small visiting area. I sat down on a vinyl couch, gazed through the glass wall separating patients from visitors and took a deep breath.

Sarah walked in with a smile on her face, as if nothing had happened. She sat down beside me and I looked at the bandage on her arm. She said, "it's nothing, just scratches."

She talked about the bland hospital food, the crazy behavior of some of the patients, the peace she felt after taking meds, the lousy programs on T.V. Before I left she turned to me and said, "Could you bring me that sweater you wear all the time? You know, the one you leave on the hook in your office?"

When I did not answer she continued, "I know I'd feel better if I could just hold onto it. Like having a piece of you right here with me."

Her wanting to have "a piece of me" made me very uncomfortable. This neediness was too much. I questioned whether giving her my sweater would be therapeutic. Wouldn't it be supporting a regressive state? Would this help her move forward? In the end, not knowing what to do, I gave it to her. If it could ease the stress of being in this place, why not?

During my second visit Sarah was upbeat, alert and animated. When she walked back onto the unit I continued to watch her through the glass wall and was amazed at how quickly her demeanor changed. With slumped shoulders, downcast eyes and shuffling gait, she took on the persona of the mental patients portrayed in *One Flew Over the Cuckoo's Nest*.

This chameleon-like transformation puzzled me and left me wondering who this person really was. Was she the wounded, misunderstood saint who had been revealed to me? Or was she one who took on whatever form was most expedite? As I would do many times in the coming months, I turned to the Bible for an answer. I found an explanation from the life of the apostle Paul, who said he became like unbelievers so that he could save some. Perhaps Sarah had acted like a mental patient in order to be able to relate with them.

Later that week the social worker asked me to send her a summary of Sarah's presenting problems and family history. I struggled over whether to describe her strange re-enactments and ended up vaguely stating that Sarah could find her own way towards mental health, even if this made no sense, as long as someone believed in her. Of course, in my mind this "someone" was me. It would be my unquestioning belief and acceptance that would bring healing. In the coming months it was this irrational belief, this need to be needed, that would prompt me to cross many more professional and personal boundaries.

The psychiatrist's diagnosis —chronic schizophrenia—sent a shock wave through me. Chronic Schizophrenia? One of the most severe mental illnesses? How could that be? That wasn't Sarah!

Looking back now, my reaction came out of the stereotypical image of an unkept man walking down the street mumbling to himself. Sarah was a college graduate, well-mannered, articulate, gentle and kind. Certainly she had shown severe disturbance, but she was not one of the *those*. Like Jesus, like Beverly, she suffered because of her special relationship with God. The secular, mental health system could not see this deeper reality as I had.

On one of my visits, Sarah gave me a cassette tape and asked me to listen to the song *You Needed Me* by Anne Murray. "It's like the song is about you. About everything you've done for me. How I feel. What you mean to me."

Paul was at work and the boys were in school when I got home. I immediately walked down to the basement, put the tape in the kid's recorder, sat down on the floor, lit up a cigarette, and listened. The song's haunting melody and powerful lyrics sung by such a deep, alto voice seeped into my soul. It transported me to a place I'd never known before:

> I cried a tear, you wiped it dry
> I was confused, you cleared my mind
> I sold my soul, you bought it back for me
> And held me up and gave me dignity . . .

And I can't believe it's you, I can't believe it's true
I needed you, and you were there
And I'll never leave, why should I leave, I'd be a fool
Cause I finally found someone who really cares

    I rewound the tape and played it over and over. Something cracked open, deep within. The lyrics filled an unexpressed longing, a vacantness. I wept. I hugged my knees. *I matter, really matter to someone. This is what I am meant for. This is why I am here.* For days, when alone, I played the song. It saddened me, invigorated me, made me feel alive.

    After Sarah's second week in the hospital the social worker called me into her office. "Sarah's depressed mood and delusional thinking have been stabilized through medication. She displays no suicidal ideation. Her insurance company will not cover any additional days in the hospital. She needs to leave."

    I was stunned. With all the presenting symptoms, with the diagnosis, I thought it would take much longer for Sarah to receive adequate treatment. The social worker continued, "I talked to Sarah about being discharged and she said she has no place to live. Do you know of anyplace?"

    The weight on my shoulders returned. She was my responsibility. After a long pause I said that maybe she could live temporarily with me and my family. The social worker jumped at the idea.

    As I talked to Paul about Sarah's desperate need to have a place to live and of my desire to help, and could we open our hearts and home to her, just for awhile, tears of compassion welled up. Perhaps that is why he agreed.

Chapter Five

We quickly set up a bedroom in the basement for the boys so Sarah could have their room. Since I was ready to terminate the few clients I was seeing and Sarah needed me with her, I decided to resign from my counseling position.

The psychiatrist knew about Sarah through our discussions about her escalating mental disturbance and subsequent hospitalization. When I told him she would be living with me and my family, he praised me for opening up my heart and home to such a needy person. He could not do this, he didn't have enough faith. This was perhaps the greatest compliment one could receive in a Christian agency that emphasized the power of faith. Receiving this from such an esteemed professional gave credence to my unorthodox treatment decision.

Sarah easily fit into the family and found her own routine. She slept late into the morning and watched M*A*S*H at four o'clock every afternoon.

Down time, with nothing planned and no expectations to meet, was what she did best. I envied her.

Sarah played checkers and Battleship with the boys, inquired about their school, cheered them on at their baseball games. She went grocery shopping with me and sometimes prepared a meal. We all liked her Hungarian goulash.

After the boys went to bed, Sarah, Paul and I often talked, drank beer and played cards. One morning Sarah jumped playfully between us while we were lying in bed, snugging up to us like a child. For a while, Paul and I were a little happier and got along better because, together, we were focused on someone besides ourselves. He was more upbeat each day when he came home from work.

During the day Sarah and I spent hours on the couch, legs stretched out, backs against the arms, smoking Benson & Hedges cigarettes (making sure to blow the smoke out the open window so Bill wouldn't know) and talking in that easy manner we'd picked up during out first lunch together. I didn't know how much I'd missed spending long, unhurried time with a friend.

It was like being in high school and meeting Georgia (my best friend since fourth grade) at the neighbors swing. One of us always brought the cigarettes, hidden in a place our parents would never find. Sitting opposite each other, we'd light up and commiserate about school and parents and boys. If we ran out of things to say we just listened to the swing gliding back and forth.

It was like an even earlier time when my younger sister and I made forts from sheets and blankets draped over upturned tables and chairs and couch cushions. Nestled in our cozy, private dwelling place, eating the crackers and Kool-Aid mom brought us, our sorority had only one rule: Our mean, bossy older brother was not allowed.

My relationship with Sarah became so consuming that it gradually edged out the rest of my life. As I was preparing to go to my weekly Bible study, Sarah became anxious. So I stayed home and never returned. Paul and I stopped going out to dinner together. I neglected the habit of taking long, solitary walks in nature. I didn't talk with God anymore. I had Sarah. And she wanted more of me.

One afternoon while we were walking in a park Sarah took hold of my hand. I was stunned, yet, not wanting to offend her, did not draw away. We kept walking hand in hand. I grew uneasy. Anyone that happened to see us would assume we were a couple. I did not see us that way.

Confused, my mind searched for an explanation and landed on Europe, where two women holding hands was a common sign of affection. Sarah, so unaffected by American mores, so natural and spontaneous, held my hand as a simple gesture of friendship. Even so, I was glad it never happened again.

Another afternoon Sarah approached me and, as I turned to face her, kissed me. When I tried pulling away she pressed in and gently flicked her tongue around my mouth. Never had I experienced such a seductive kiss. It captivated me. I could not move.

"Wow, where'd you learn to kiss that way?" I asked, after she pulled away, for I figured this kind of kiss must have been practiced.

"I guess it's just instinctual" she replied, then added, "I can show you a different way, a better way of loving."

A part of me quickly grasped that what she was referring to was sexual. But another part immediately rejected this. If this were true, all that I had come to believe, all I had given my life to, was a lie. *No, that can't be what she means! We are God's chosen ones. Our relationship is spiritual, not of this world, higher than merely physical.*

I did not ask Sarah to elaborate nor to show me a different, a better way of loving. Instead, I spiritualized her comment. *Yes, to this saint God has revealed a secret, higher form of love. Maybe someday I'll experience it, too.*

Our conversations became more intimate. Sarah asked "What's the worse thing you've ever done? The thing you feel most guilty about?"

It didn't take long to come up with the most shameful thing I'd ever done. I struggled over whether I could say it, then began. "I'm not sure how old I was, maybe eight or nine." I paused, then continued. "I was sleeping over at a friends' house. When I knew she was asleep I touched her panties and started to rub her, you know, between her legs. I just wanted to see what would happen. Then I got scared she'd wake up and stopped. I knew it was wrong. I felt like such a bad person."

I took a breath and said, "Wow, I've never told anyone about that."

I was relieved when Sarah did not react in horror or revulsion but said, "I think all kids are naturally curious about sex. There's all kinds of different ways to experiment with it."

This was not new to me. My sexual views had broadened with the times. Yet to hear a saintly woman's view helped loosen the moral code I'd absorbed through family and church in the 1950s: any and all sexual contact outside of marriage between a man and woman is reprehensible — the worse kind of sin.

Sarah then disclosed some of the sexual things she and her cousins had done. Such a frank conversation around a forbidden subject was like opening a window to let in fresh air. It also opened a Pandora's box.

Sarah began speaking about her greatest unfulfilled desire.

"You know, I have never felt anything down there, where my cousin hurt me. It feels dead. If I could just have an orgasm, feel something, anything."

"Having an orgasm is not the be-all, end-all you think it is," I said.

"But if I could just feel this, if you could touch this place that's so dead, bring it to life, I think I could be healed."

"Isn't knowing God intimately, the way you do, enough?" I asked.

"No. I really need to feel the physical touch of a person."

"You could stimulate yourself."

"No, I just can't do that. The Catholic church says it is wrong."

I pressed on. "You'll get married someday. Then you'll experience sex in a loving way, with your husband."

"I'm getting too old. Past the age of meeting anyone. I don't think that will ever happen. I don't know what else to do. Where to turn. Would you, please?"

How could I refuse? She needed me. This was part of her healing. She knew best. I believed in her. To stay by her, to sacrifice for her — this is what I had been appointed for, this was my life's mission. I agreed.

Sarah took off her underwear and laid down on the bed. I approached her, hesitated and said, "I don't think I can do this."

"Sure you can. Go ahead. It's alright."

With the mindset of an emotionally detached surgeon I touched her and was surprised she was already moist. I turned my head away and, following her instruction, moved my fingers around her labia and vagina. She remained motionless, unresponsive. The next day Sarah asked me to try again. I did. When it became obvious this was not going to result in any kind of arousal we agreed to stop the "procedure."

It took years before I discarded the spiritual/clinical language I had framed this experience in and set it alongside the sexual acts I did with high school boys. Like Sarah, these boys pleaded with me to relieve their suffering by rubbing them. Each time I consented, (there were only a few times, yet it felt like a multitude) I gave up a piece of myself and was left feeling used, dirty and ashamed.

Even though Sarah never experienced any feelings "down there" I continued to believe God had appointed me as her healer. Unlike the people who had turned against her or let her down – her family, the leaders of her Christian community, the psychotherapists – I would not. All it took was one person to believe in her, stand by her, never give up on her.

"I am your salvation," I blurted out one afternoon. As soon as the words were out, I rejected them. *What am I saying? I know salvation comes only through Jesus Christ!* Yet that sudden, unexpected declaration, erupting from a deep place, spoken with such conviction, revealed what I really believed.

By the time Sarah had been in our home for three months my life was strapped to hers. Of course, being so consumed with her caused rifts in my marriage. One late afternoon, at the conclusion of a heated argument, Paul insisted that Sarah leave. Since I could not, would not, desert her, the only thing to do was leave with her. I told Sarah to pack her things, I'd meet her in the car.

I called Matthew and Andrew to the bedroom. Taking hold of their hands I looked into their faces and said, "I'm going away for a while."

"Can we go too?" Andrew asked.

"No, you'll stay here with dad. He'll take good care of you. You need to stay in school. You want to keep playing baseball, right?"

"When will you be back?" asked Matthew.

"I'm not sure." As his head dropped I added, "I know that's hard to hear. I'm sorry. I love you guys. You know that, right? I'll always love you. Let's have a group squeeze okay?"

With Paul standing in the hallway silently looking on, I threw some clothes into a suitcase. Standing in front of my dresser, I thought, *can I leave Matthew and Andrew? Is this really God's will for me?* I paused, giving God a chance to tell me with some word or sign not to go, but felt assured the boys would be all right without me. They had their dad. I picked up the suitcase and walked out the door.

Chapter Six

We headed east on Interstate 94. Sarah drove. The sky was a dreary, dull grey. On the northern horizon dark clouds were forming (or perhaps this "memory" is only a reflection of what was to come). I felt numb and stared out the side window. Sarah lit up a cigarette. "What's wrong?" she asked.

"I'm not so sure this is the right thing to do. We don't have any place to go. You know, maybe I can work things out with Paul."

"Let's just find a motel, relax a little and talk things out in the morning, ok?"

"Yah, that'd be okay. Turn off here. I see a motel over there."

The motel had a *No Vacancies* sign out front so we continued on and found ourselves aimlessly driving around a run down commercial district. Finally spotting a bright blue motel with a half burned out flashing neon sign we decided this would have to do. When I signed the register I felt anxious, and as trashy as the motel. Checking into a motel with someone other than my husband felt wrong. Like I was in another relationship. *But we weren't a couple, at least not in that way. Did we look like it? What did this man at the desk think?*

As I write this another question arises. How did we pay for the motel, along with other expenses occurred along the way, like gas and food?

Paul controlled our finances. I turned my small paycheck over to him. I had no major credit card, no checking account in my name. When I asked Paul for spending money he often gave me flak, which made me feel like a dependent child, so whenever I wrote a check, I made it for more than what I'd purchased so I could pocket the extra cash. Sarah must have paid for everything. I don't recall feeling guilty about that.

After finding our motel room and checking for bugs, we plopped down on our beds. In a little while, Sarah's breathing became heavy and her pelvis started to gyrate. When I asked her what was happening she said, "Beams of light are coming into me. Massaging me. Oh, Jesus, you're here! In me! Thank-you. Thank-you."

Thinking it improper to watch such intimacy, I turned my head away. *This is ridiculous, degrading. This is not the Jesus portrayed in the Bible.*

When it was over Sarah turned to me and said, "This has happened before. I can't explain it. It's just how Jesus comes to me, a way of being united with Him."

Wanting — needing — to trust her, I put my doubts aside and found a place for this alongside other beliefs I held about her and God. *Sarah has experienced God's presence — God's love — in inexplicable, extraordinary ways. Who am I to question how God chooses to come to her? His ways are above and beyond all human comprehension.*

In the morning Sarah said she had an uncle and aunt who lived in a suburb of Chicago and maybe we could stay with them for a while. I agreed and with Sarah driving, we set off, a pack of cigarettes on the dashboard between us.

I stretched out and laid my head on Sarah's lap. She began to utter a kind of gibberish that was not altogether strange. In the pentecostal community I had been part of as well as the charismatic community Sarah had lived in, speaking in an unknown language was a means of prayer and worship. When I was alone I had even practiced speaking 'in tongues.'

As I listened to Sarah's gibberish my body started to jerk. My arms thrust out, my legs kicked. Sarah kept chanting. My torso convulsed like someone having a seizure. I felt as limp and lifeless as a rag doll being tossed about. It lasted about a minute or two and when it stopped my head was on the seat and the rest of my body was on the floor.

I was rattled by the thrashing. And puzzled. *What could this have been? What did it mean?* I do not remember talking to Sarah about it, although it seems incredulous that we did not.

What I remember was coming up with one more explanation. This was the Holy Spirit within me acknowledging her spirt and, like Elizabeth's unborn child leaping for joy in the presence of Jesus. Yet, in spite of this explanation, doubt lingered. *Then why did I feel jerked around and controlled? Not at all joyful?*

I cannot recall whether Sarah phoned her uncle and aunt before we arrived. They graciously took us into their clean, well-decorated, thickly carpeted home. We slept in the spare bedroom upstairs. Since her uncle and aunt worked during the day, evenings were the only time we saw them. I hope Sarah and I helped prepare meals but I cannot say for sure. We were so immersed in our own private world.

Sitting on twin beds, our backs propped against the wall, Sarah and I chatted easily as we drank our wine. Turning my head toward her I noticed how attractive her breasts were. Firm, round, not too big, not too small. Sarah sensed I was looking at her and said, "Would you like to touch my breasts?"

I said, "No, not in that way." But then another thought entered my mind. "You know, I never felt loved or wanted by my mother. So maybe I could go there as an infant, feeding at her, um, you know, a mother's breast. Maybe experience that very first, innocent bond, the love that only a mother can provide."

She said, "I will be this mother for you."

This is the epitome of Godliness I thought. *Willing to offer so much of herself, to give everything she has. Such sacrificial love.*

I laid down beside Sarah and began to gently suck at her breast. *This is not right!* I immediately felt a sharp contraction in the pit of my stomach. I tried to relax, to ignore the *I know what this looks like,* to somehow erase my adult conscience. After more tries the stomach contractions eased, yet I never got beyond the here and now, never felt the bliss of pure love. The experiment was a failure. All it did was make me feel more guilty.

In spite of the failures with Sarah, I continued to believe we were onto some cutting-edge discoveries in the healing of deep emotional and psychic wounds. I fantasized about becoming renown throughout the professional world. But when I considered how to write about this particular intervention method so that other mental health professionals might duplicate it, the illusion faded.

When Sarah's aunt asked to speak with us, I knew something was up. Seated at the dining room table, her husband at her side, she began. "Sarah, you know we've always loved you and are glad you came here when you had nowhere else to go. But this cannot go on. I don't think you've looked for any kind of work, have you?" Sarah looked down and shook her head. I felt a fissure crack in our little world.

"Have you thought about how you might support yourselves? Do you have any kind of financial plan?" Surprised by the utter reasonableness of her inquiry, the fissure grew wider. "I'm sorry, we cannot continue supporting you. It's not good for us, or for you." Her words were spoken with such tenderness it took me a moment to realize we'd just been booted out.

We packed our clothes, expressed our thanks and walked to the car. I turned to Sarah and asked, "What are we going to do now?"

"I don't know," Sarah replied.

Then it hit me. *We were homeless!* How did this happen? This can't be!

Searching for any kind of solution, my mind landed on Aunt Myrtle. A large, freckled faced woman with a sunny disposition, she and her two boys spent time at the lake with my family every summer. I had not seen Aunt Myrtle since graduating from college.

Somehow I remembered the Florida town she now lived in, found her phone number from directory assistance and called. How are the boys?

How's your health? Do you like living there? I'm on a little vacation with a friend, exploring new places, could we come and stay with you a few days?

"No, dear, I think you should go back home. But thanks for calling. It was so nice to hear from you."

I thanked her, hung up and became livid. It was obvious that Bill had already called, alerting her to his run-away wife.

We were stuck. I could not go back to Paul, we could not spend our lives in motels, we were running out of money and knew of no one who could take us in. The only thing left was to go to my parent's home in Rauma, Ohio, where I grew up.

Chapter Seven

I drove across Indiana so Sarah could sleep. As we passed the college I had attended I found myself reflecting on all the important decisions I'd made there. I had really wanted to be a nurse, but was afraid I'd flunk the science classes — too much memorization. I had thought about becoming a physical education teacher but figured that would be too frivolous, too enjoyable, too selfish. So, as a means of helping others, I chose social work.

I met Paul during my senior year and married him because he had broad shoulders and was youth director in a church. Even more importantly, I married him because I needed a place to live. All my roommates had different plans, I could not fathom living alone, and returning to my parents home was not an option.

As I continued driving, I found myself thinking about the moral skirmish that had plagued me for so long. Was our physical contact sexual? clinical? I had always believed it was a means of healing. Then why did it feel so wrong? How could I know what was right?

I decided to bring it up with Sarah. Perhaps she had also felt pangs of guilt or confusion. Between us, maybe we could find the right way.

I considered how to broach the subject. When Sarah woke up I began, "This is hard to talk about, but I don't know what else to do. Sometimes I'm not sure what we're doing, you know, physically, with each other, is right. How about whenever one of us is feeling even a little guilty and thinks something is wrong, we agree to stop and follow her lead? You know, like the Bible says, go along with the one who is weaker in faith."

Sarah said nothing.

"What do you think?" I asked.

Sarah looked down and said, "I don't know what you're talking about." After a moment she added, "But if that's what you need, I'll go along with it."

This moment was very significant. At a time when I had compromised so much, when I had violated my conscience so many times, I was still able to act from an innermost place that knew what was right for me. It was not weakness that nudged me to bring this up to Sarah as I had thought at the time, it was a sense of power — of integrity. "And the darkness did not overcome it" (John 1:5)

When we went by the second university I had attended I spoke about the whim of applying to graduate school after Paul completed his bachelor's degree, the surprise of being accepted, the wonder of discovering I could be a good student, the places Paul and I lived. Sarah gazed out the window.

An hour from my parent's house I figured I should call and let them know I was coming, but I wasn't sure which exit to take, where to find a public phone booth or what to say. I suppose fear was at the bottom of this – fear of having to explain myself, fear of being turned away. I calculated that just showing up was the best bet.

When we arrived I knocked instead of walking in as I normally did. Mom came to the kitchen door, smiled and said, "Oh, Eileen, come on in. Just a sec. I was just finishing dinner."

She quickly molded the meatloaf into a pan, wiped off her hands, hugged me, looked at Sarah and before I could introduce her said, "You must be Sarah, so nice to finally meet you," and clasped both her hands.

Dad walked into the kitchen, looked at me, then at Sarah then back at me. Sarah shook his hand. When he extended it to me I walked toward him, softly nestled my face next to his shoulder and said, "I'm sorry Dad." Now, as I rethink this sweet connection and apology, I'm not quite sure it actually happened, although it might have and I hope it did.

After some strained attempts at small talk about how our drive went, Dad went back to the living room to watch the evening news and Mom put the meatloaf in the oven. Sarah said she wasn't feeling well so I took her to the bedroom my sister and I had shared so many years ago. When she laid down I felt disjointed, like I was in the middle of two different worlds. I tried to stifle the thought that she didn't belong here, that she was a trespasser lying on the bed where my sister and I had innocently shared secrets and butterfly kisses before going to sleep.

Mom was standing just outside the bedroom when I came. We walked into the family room and she asked about Sarah. I said, "She has so many problems. Her family doesn't understand her. She spent some time in a psychiatric hospital and was diagnosed with schizophrenia. I just want to help her. She has nowhere to go, no one she trusts but me. But it's been hard on me. Caring about her, you know. Being with her, feeling so responsible for her."

Mom quietly listened, nodded, then left to fetch some aspirin.

One of the most important things in my family was taking care of others, especially of mom, who was emotionally fragile. According to my brother, mom had a 'nervous breakdown' when we were quite young and we lived with gramma for awhile. I have no recollection of this.

When not parenting small children Mom was gentle and compassionate — a trusting person who believed the best in others. (She even believed the lies I told when I came home after high school dates, disheveled and drunk.) So when I relayed Sarah's problems and the hardship of being her caregiver she gave me what I needed — understanding and sympathy.

After giving Sarah the aspirin, Mom stayed in the room for quite a while. I got a little worried and when I looked in she was sitting on the bed, head bent toward Sarah, talking softly. I felt relieved to have someone else attend to Sarah, yet also felt a sense of duplicity in the way I had drawn

Mom in and a vague fear about what Sarah might say — about how Sarah might influence her. I knew how naive and gullible Mom could be.

Trying to get acclimated, to clear my mind, I looked around the house. A new light blue curtain covered a window that divided the house in two — a window that had been on the outside of the little house before the addition was added.

Us kids loved to tell every visitor about how our house came to be. About our richest neighbor (an older couple with no children) selling the little house to our parents for a dollar. About a flat bed truck moving it to our property, a half mile away, as kids ran alongside it and adults stood around cheering. About the addition being built mostly by skilled neighborhood men. I remember how impressed I was when I saw my thirteen year old brother working alongside them, no longer a boy.

I noticed the same Reader's Digest Condensed books on the bookshelf, along with some ancient classics no one ever read. The faded landscapes with plastic frames still hung on the walls. A new yellow and orange flowered oilcloth, with tape holding it down, covered the dining room table.

In the living room, on the other side of the curtain, stood a cord organ Mom played most days, often with jibs from us kids to "Stop!" or "Turn on the soft pedal!" I think we probably did the same thing when she played the used, freshly painted piano dad bought her when we first moved into the house.

Early the next morning Dad was already at work slicing an onion for the split pea soup. It would simmer all afternoon. Later that day my brother, David, his wife Mia, and their three children came for the usual Saturday sauna and supper. About an hour later my sister, Pamela, her husband Will, and their four children arrived.

Sarah was stiffly polite when introduced to them and remained unusually quiet throughout the day, often retreating to the bedroom. When I asked if she felt overwhelmed in being around so many noisy children and adults she said she was just tired. I now wonder if she felt resentment from family members who blamed her for leading one of their own astray.

When David and Will finished their sauna they sauntered to the table wearing thick, white bathrobes. Their three red-cheeked, glowing sons trotted behind. I automatically looked for my sons. *Where are Matthew and Andrew?* Almost as quickly as the question crossed my mind, another thought supplanted it. *They are not here.* I gasped. It literally felt like the right side of my body was missing.

Mia, not wanting to miss out on sauna time, went in the sauna next. Pam rounded up her three girls and asked if I was coming. Having missed out on many sauna gatherings since moving away from home, I wanted to join in. But there was Sarah.

When I asked if she wanted to take a sauna, Sarah said she wasn't up for it. Because the Finnish custom is to sauna in the buff with those of the same sex, and I thought this might be uncomfortable for her, I said we could wear swimsuits. She declined. I never did take that sauna, and still regret missing out on a family tradition where all the women and girls sat side by on a wooden bench, breathing in the cleansing heat and easy conversation.

As David was getting ready to leave he pulled me aside and asked to speak with me outside. We walked around the house and stood outside my parents' bedroom window. He looked at me. "Mom and Dad don't want you here. Don't you know how much you've disrupted their life? Do you have any idea how upset they are?" He paused. "This is just like you! Always making trouble."

To be thrown back into a family role I had not played for twenty years stunned me into silence. I wondered how it was that, after all these years of having a life completely separate from theirs, I was still seen as the troublemaker. And why was David speaking for them? How had he come to be their protector? Why couldn't they speak for themselves?

I quickly regained my ability to speak and told David I was unaware of the turmoil I was causing, apologized and said I'd be leaving soon.

After dinner that night, Sarah excused herself and went to lie down. As we finished our dessert, Dad and I had a conversation that went something like this:

Dad: Are you ready to go back? Where you belong? With your husband and children?

Me: Yeah, but sometimes it's hard living with Paul.

Dad: He doesn't hit you or abuse you, does he?

Me: No. There was just that time, when we were engaged, when he got mad at me and slammed the canoe paddle down, bending the bar in the middle. Remember? Everyone joked about it. But it scared me. That paddle could have landed on my head!

Dad: But it didn't, right?

Me: Yeah, that's right. But Paul can get so irritated at the smallest thing. I try to please him but nothing seems good enough. We never really talk.

Dad: All marriages have hard times. You know you have to go back. I'm sure you and Paul can work out your differences. Matthew and Andrew need you.

Me: I know, I know. Sarah and I will leave in the morning.

So it was finally Dad, with his gentle, persistent, no nonsense approach who convinced me to return home. How I wish he could have talked to me like that when I was fifteen, stuck in a maze of booze and boys, in need of a father's strong, loving hand. But back then Dad and I had few interactions without one of us, usually me, flaring up.

Chapter Eight

I thought about taking Sarah to Eagle Lake before we returned to Eau Claire. Surrounded by trees, the lake had a grassy picnic area with a community sauna, a small playground, a sandy beach, a roped off swimming area and two docks – one for fishing and the other with a tall, two platform tower for diving or jumping into the lake below. The lake was small yet not too small and very deep. Underground spring water created patches of cold which always surprised you and made your spine tingle.

Eagle Lake is where I first remember being noticed. I was five and the swimming instructor asked me to demonstrate treading water to the rest of the class. It felt strange to be singled out for doing something good, but after it happened a few more times, I relished the spotlight. In a small way, I felt chosen. Later, I was one of a few girls to master the high dive and lapped up the accolades this drew from friends and spectators watching from shore.

I lived for summers and spent them with a small group of friends whose families migrated from their city homes to live in one-room, rustic cabins near Eagle Lake. When they went back to the city, I went to the lake. Whenever I was bored or restless, spring or fall, I walked the mile from my house to the lake. Standing at the end of the dock, looking out at the rippling water and pristine shoreline, feeling the soft breeze on my face, I knew I was home.

I did not take Sarah to Eagle Lake.

The drive back to Wisconsin was uneventful, with only scattered bits of conversation. There was not much to say. I felt deflated and scared. Our run-away had lasted only eleven days, yet felt like years. After dropping me off, Sarah went back to her mother's and I readied myself to meet my family.

When I entered the house, Paul was noticeably relieved and unusually reserved. I cannot recall if the boys hung back or rushed to greet me or acted as if there was nothing unusual about my arrival (which I would like to believe). What I do remember is that as we hugged, I felt a strong dose of remorse. Holding back my tears, I told them I was sorry for leaving. Andrew assured me that it was okay. He always knew I'd be back. I was overwhelmed at his trust in me, a trust I didn't deserve.

I quickly resumed the cooking and cleaning I'd done through the years, yet often felt numb or spacey. Being around Matthew and Andrew brought a sense of normalcy and I breathed in their freshness and liveliness. Matthew stayed home more than usual, often staying in the room I was in, watching. Andrew seemed unaffected and carried on as if nothing unusual had happened.

Paul and I did not talk much. He never asked about anything that happened while I was gone. I never initiated anything. I promised not to see Sarah again, but found I could not refuse her pleas, "just to see you, to talk for awhile."

One day we were at her mother's house and went up to the attic in search of something. I playfully laid down on a bunch of clothing bags. Sarah walked over, climbed on top of me, and began humping. I thought it funny, her mimic of a crude, clumsy guy trying to have his way with me.

She pinned down my arms and rubbed harder against me. I was stunned. "Stop it!" I yelled.

"Just relax," she said.

I struggled. I became aroused. Sarah noticed her mother standing by the doorway. Sarah got off me and her mother walked away.

"What was that all about? Why'd you do that?" I asked.

"I thought that's what you liked," she replied.

I was astonished at how little she knew me. This couldn't be further from the truth. The incident finally crushed any remaining belief that Sarah was some kind of saint, that our sexual encounters were a unique method to heal childhood wounds. It also left me wondering if becoming sexually aroused meant I was a lesbian. It took years before I realized that a body does not recognize whether feeling sexually stimulated came from a man or a woman.

On a clear, sunny day in July, I took a long walk through the neighborhood and ended up at Long Lake. Strolling along the beach, breathing in the air, savoring the solitude, my thoughts turned to Sarah. Suddenly I felt trapped, suffocated. Sarah's need to be with me was smothering. Our relationship was stagnant. It was going nowhere. It smelled bad.

I thought about ending it, yet how could I? God had called me to this. Somehow my presence would heal her, even if I could not see how. Following God's will was not always easy – it required sacrifice, bearing burdens, enduring till the end. What would she do, how could she live without me?

In August I told Sarah my family was driving to Ohio to visit my parents. I was also looking forward to spending a little time with some friends. Her hands began to fidget.

"You aren't coming back to me, are you?" she said. I reassured her that I would be back, but the words sounded hollow.

Chapter Nine

It was good to see Beverly, Janet, and Pat again. We sat in Janet's living room drinking iced tea, commiserating about husbands who had yet to see the light and turn to the Lord. Not much had changed in the past four years. Beverly was leading another Bible study and was about to release a new album. I was eager to tell them about the healing ministry God had called me to. Just as I was about to speak I heard the words *Tell All,* spoken clearly within.

I described Sarah's difficulties, hospitalization and diagnosis, of my desire to help in any way I could, of seeing her as a wounded saint in need of healing, of taking her into my home, of leaving after Paul no longer wanted her there. I was reluctant to tell about the physically intimate parts – I knew what this looked like – but I had a God-given directive and plunged on.

As I spoke I felt a veil being lifted from my eyes. Everything about Sarah and me was cast in a different light. I felt horribly embarrassed.

When I finished I knew I had been no specially called servant of God. I had been deceived.

There was silence for what seemed like a long time. Then Beverly declared, "Sarah is demon-possessed."

She paused, "And you are demon possessed. Scripture clearly states that it is possible for a Christian to be oppressed by demons, but never possessed, so you are not a Christian."

I tried to take in what she said. Yes, I could agree I was possessed, that the awful things I'd done had been the work of some evil force. Not being a Christian was harder to take. Like a rushing waterfall, evidence of my relationship with God cascaded through my mind: surrendering my life to God, being baptized (twice), receiving the baptism of the Holy Spirit, feeling God's presence and wondering how to tell others, desiring to follow the Lord, wherever he led. Were all these false? A sham?

In the end, even with all this internal evidence, I accepted Beverly's verdict. After all, she was the expert in such matters. *She's right,* I thought. *How could a Christian go so far astray? Desert her children? Do such immoral things?*

Beverly continued, "I know a godly woman of prayer who is known for her ministry of casting out demons. Would you like me to phone her?"

I nodded, yet felt dubious about this whole demon business. Beverly called and after a private, lengthy conversation came back and said Mary would be available at 10:00 the following morning. We would all meet at Beverly's.

The next day when Pat, Janet and I arrived, Beverly immediately went downstairs to calm her dog, who was nervously pacing the floor and barking.

"This is so unusual for her," Beverly casually remarked when she returned. "Could be her animal instinct kicking in, reacting to the evil that is present."

I thought that the idea of a dog reacting to an evil force flying around in the air was ridiculous. I almost laughed, until another part of me considered that it is me who is the carrier of that evil. How repugnant I must be if a dog can't stand being near me.

Mary arrived and after brief introductions nudged closer to me, fixed her eyes on my face and asked if I wanted to be delivered. I acknowledged that I did. Mary said I must first become a Christian, so with her prompts, I acknowledged my sin, renounced Satan and all his forces and asked Jesus to come into my life as Lord and Savior. I couldn't help comparing this rote prayer to the heart felt, treacherous prayer I had uttered ten years before as I hurled myself into the abyss and shouted *Okay, God, you've got me!*

Mary placed her hands on my head and in the name of Jesus commanded the demons to leave. Nothing happened. Beverly placed her hands on my head. Mary prayed in tongues. She commanded the demon to state its name. Nothing was said. She conversed with Beverly about a legion of demons and offered some kind of explanation as to why they were silent. I thought it odd to be talked about as if I wasn't present, yet kept silent. Mary asked the others to place their hands on me and pray. I began to pray silently. *God, please help me. God, please help me.*

Suddenly I was jerked off the sofa, just as I had been thrust around in the car, and found myself sitting on the floor. The women surrounded me and kept praying. My body flattened out on the floor and became rigid. I thought I could get up if I wanted, but decided to remain on the floor, not to fight whatever was happening to me, to take it to the end.

My only fear was going crazy and I thought, *If I can just keep thinking, tracking all that is going on, I'll be alright, I won't lose my mind.* So, lying on the floor, with my eyes closed, with a curious, detached mind, I vigilantly listened to all that was going on within and around me.

My breath became more shallow and rapid, like when I was in labor. Mary encouraged me to breathe more deeply, explaining that the spirits were being expelled. As I focused on controlling my breath my body gradually relaxed while my mind kept its vigilance. When my breath returned to normal Mary pronounced all evil spirits gone. The exorcist lasted perhaps twenty minutes. Contrary to films like *The Exorcist,* there was no head revolving, no body levitating.

Afterwards, sitting in the back seat of the car with Pat and Janet, no one spoke. What was there to say? "My, that was a fine exorcism wasn't it?" I think we were all stunned. I was not certain that anything had happened.

I felt no different — no sense of relief, of lightness or clarity, of coming into my right mind. Only confusion. Had I actually been demon possessed? Yet, there had been those body contractions. What was that all about? If this had been the movement of demons I was worried about whether they had all been expelled. If they would return. Maybe Janet and Pat were too.

In spite of these fears, Janet and Pat showed no fear in playing an active part in my deliverance. They read the letters Sarah had written to me. Pat had such a visceral reaction to their contents that she burned them. Both advised – no directed – me to have no further contact with Sarah, to engage in no conversation with her. None. Because they were so uncharacteristically firm, I trusted their judgement (mine was a bit tattered) and promised to follow their directive.

When my family returned home Sarah kept calling. I did not veer from the line I had memorized. "I'm sorry, I cannot see you anymore." No matter what she said, no matter what question or objection she started to raise, I repeated the line and promptly hung up. Then felt guilty. *How could I do that? Hurt her like that? Be so mean?* But then I'd recall the promise I had given to two trusted friends.

I felt relieved when Sarah stopped calling, yet my inner turmoil did not stop. Like a slide projector, my mind repeatedly viewed scene after scene, trying to find connections, to make sense of it all. *How could I have been so wrong when all I wanted was to do God's will? God, where were you? Why didn't you stop me?*

Then I remembered the prophetic words that had impressed themselves upon me several months before: *This will end one day.* In the crux of the relationship, thick with confusion, unable to move, they were like a dim light at the end of a dark tunnel. I could not fathom how this could ever be, yet held onto the promise. The promise had been kept. It was over.

Chapter Ten

Even though it was over, everything I had based my life on was shattered, like shards of broken glass. I felt suspended in midair, tethered to nothing. Doing things for the family helped, but it was not enough. I had too much time to dwell on the past. I became certain of only two things: It was not good for me to be alone and I needed help to focus on something besides myself.

Pat told me about a lay school for adults who wanted in-depth Christian education along with time to discern their career path or calling. I applied six weeks before school was to start. When the acceptance letter came, I was shocked they would let in someone like me, then relieved and excited. For the next nine months I would have someplace to go, people to be with.

Somehow I convinced Paul. Perhaps he went along because he was afraid I might leave home or reality again if I didn't get my way. He made it clear that he was not keen on paying for tuition. Besides that, Paul was a hard line traditionalist and, even though the school was Lutheran, he might have been afraid of its charismatic leanings.

Charismatics of all stripes – whether officially Pentecostal or not – were more spontaneous and emotional than mainline churchgoers. It was common to raise hands, close eyes, clap, sway and even smile. People sometimes spoke in tongues, often followed by an interpretation in English.

On the first day of class, everything was laid out for us. Besides attending class every morning, students were expected to meet with a mentor (second year student) and small group, read scripture and books on the Christian life, pray and journal daily, take exams, write papers, and record personal and spiritual growth. Besides being *somewhere*, I had not really considered that school meant work. I wasn't sure my mind could handle it.

I felt like an imposter until, during a break, the young woman sitting in front of me turned around and said, "Hi, I'm Sue Wheaton. Oh, yeah, you can see that on my name tag." She giggled. "And you're Eileen Turner!" We're in the same cluster. With Donna. Her husband is doing his internship here. He's super smart."

Sue scooted her chair close to my table, rested her chin on top of her hands, looked up at me with big, brown eyes and continued. "JoAnn is in our cluster too. We room together. In the apartments across the street. Where do you live?" She smiled broadly.

I smiled back. "I live about fifteen miles away, with my husband and two sons."

The director called us back and Sue returned to her table, yet her presence stayed with me. Such a friendly, spontaneous, chatty introduction had acted as a bridge that brought me back into the human fold. Many such bridges would be crossed that year.

The lay school quickly became not so much a place of learning as a place of healing. Having a daily structure I could count on grounded me. Meeting class expectations forced me to concentrate on something besides myself. Being with others gave me a sense of normalcy. But it was hard. There was too much social buzzing going on around me. I felt distracted and could not stay focused for very long.

Being part of a small group that met every Friday morning became the highlight of the week. We were a lively, honest bunch of four women. At thirty-eight, I was the oldest. Blurting out anything that crossed her mind, Sue seemed unaware of how funny she could be – unaware of what a gift this was to someone who hadn't laughed in some time.

Joann was more reserved yet quick to find the humor in any situation. She struggled over whether to become a pastor. Toward the end of the year she announced her decision to attend seminary. I had mixed feelings. I didn't think she emitted enough confidence to carry out such a public role. Even though the American Lutheran Church had ordained women since 1970, I had never known a female pastor and, although I would never admit it, believed men were the only ones qualified to hold such a high position.

Donna was a second-year student who did not try to direct us too much. She may have gleaned early on just how impossible that would be. During our individual meetings I often spoke about the problems that were escalating between Paul and me.

When I felt angry or sad Donna played her guitar and sang gentle worship songs to try to make me feel better. I appreciated her attempts to help, yet I did not want to feel better. I wanted someone to listen and understand what I was going through.

During the school year my relationship with God changed profoundly. My identity gradually shifted from being chosen to being human. Whereas before, my perceived relationship with God inflated my ego, took me outside of myself and separated me from others, now encounters with God humbled me and brought me into an authenticity I had never experienced before.

In a morning worship service, a passage was read from Isaiah 49: "The Lord has forsaken me. He has forgotten me." I was right there, this was me. I felt the devastating ache of being left alone. "Can a woman forget her nursing child, and have no compassion for the son of her womb?" This sudden shift hit me hard, refuting what I was feeling. No, God is like a woman nursing her child. As I entered into sensations I experienced while nursing my babies – tender, loving, gentle feelings like none other – I felt the same mother love being poured into me. I cried unabashedly.

At the end of September, the class went on a weekend retreat. Held at a beautiful conference center beside a small lake, the only requirement was that, other than brief presentations by staff, there would be no talking.

Saturday was a stellar day with a gentle breeze, bright blue sky and wispy white clouds. I spent the afternoon slowly walking up and down the grassy hills, taking in all the beauty and vitality around me. As I walked, my breathing gradually slowed and deepened.

I brought my mind back to the question we were asked to meditate on: "Do you love me more than these?" *More than these* was too much for my tired mind so I shortened it to *Do you love me?* As I kept rolling this around in my mind I felt a sudden rush of emotion and cried out *God, I love You. God I love You! You're here! God I love you, I've always loved you!*

I walked over to the lake and sat down on an old pontoon boat. Gazing out on gently rippling water, I again spoke inwardly to God. *You were there with me at Eagle Lake, too, weren't you?* In my mind's eye I saw myself as a teenage girl lying on the fishing dock, an unopened novel by my side. I felt the sun penetrate my back, my shoulders, my arms, and understood this to be the summer after graduating from high school.

In a few short months I would set off for college. On that dock it dawned on me that when I left home I could finally leave my bad reputation behind. No more binge drinking, or letting boys go too far, or throwing wild pajama parties. No more need to present a bravado, daring persona. When I left home my life could start anew.

But I was not alone on that dock. In my mind's eye, I saw a man dressed in white pants rolled up to his knees sitting on the edge of the dock, swishing his feet in the water. He was relaxed and carefree, yet sensitive and attentive to all that was going on around him. I knew this was Jesus. He was not anxious to be someplace else, to be doing something more important. All of him was there on the dock, with me. And the most remarkable thing was that Jesus asked nothing of me but to be there with Him.

As the day continued, I moved not only more deeply into silence, but also into community. During dinner, as we acknowledged one another through eye contact, I felt an unusual sense of peace, of belonging. There was no pressure to talk. We were all in this quiet space together. No one stood out, no one faded away. The retreat ended way too soon. I did not want to come out of the liberating silence.

One morning I slept in and had no time to mediate on the assigned scripture passage. While driving to school I decided to give it a go and, even though I knew it was a bad idea, propped my Bible up on the steering wheel. "You did not choose me, but I chose you, and appointed you, that you should go and bear fruit, and that your fruit should remain, that whatever you ask of the Father in My name, He may give to you."

I slowly repeated every phrase. As I came to *whatever . . you . . ask*, it was as if the heavens opened and I clearly heard a voice, not with my ears, but in a deep hidden place say, *Eileen, what is it you wish to ask of me?* In my imagination I saw a blank check and knew I could fill it out with whatever I chose.

It took a moment for the answer to come. *Friends, Lord, I want friends! Lots and lots of friends!* This took me by surprise, probably because it expressed such a common human need and I had grown accustomed to thinking of myself as rather extraordinary. Yet I knew my prayer was spot on. Friends are what I most wanted, what I desperately missed since leaving that band of Bible believing women.

Beth taught Prayer and Meditation and became the favorite instructor of many students, including me. When she walked into the classroom, a lightness and freshness – like spring air – blew in with her. With a laid back manner, dry sense of humor, and subtle defiance of organized religion, she taught about prayer that emptied the mind and went deeper than words. Using people like third-century Saint Theresa and thirteenth-century St. John of the Cross, she taught of a mystical union where a person was so caught up in God she lost a sense of self. I wanted to be lost in God. But I was terrified of losing my sense of self.

I felt anxious when filling out the self-evaluation I handed to Donna each week. One question was *Have you had an experiential awareness of God's presence in your mediation/journaling/prayer? Please describe.* Emotion was my litmus test so whenever I experienced notable feelings I happily wrote about them. More often, however, I felt bored and distracted during meditation and prayer and blamed myself. I hadn't done it right, wasn't fervent enough, should try harder, stay longer.

With Joann's encouragement, I started attending the contemplative prayer gatherings headed by Beth. If in high school being a cheerleader was the highest form of social status, certainly this was the highest status a Christian could attain. Yet, I was perpetually frustrated sitting in silence with others, trying to quiet my mind. Convinced a deeper commitment was needed, I decided to become a member.

As I was about to take this next step, I awakened in the middle of the night and heard, so clearly it was almost audible, *Don't go.* Nothing else had to be said. I knew it was God directing me not to enter the community, just as it was God who directed me to *Tell All* to my Ohio friends. Relieved, I withdrew from the group.

Today, I realize my life would have turned out much differently had I joined. I believe God turned me away from a community which would have molded me into something that did not fit who I was and would become. Had I joined, I would have retreated from the world again, rather than becoming actively engaged in it.

The director of the school was a brilliant, articulate, intimidating man who taught a class on the Old Testament. As the school year was about to end, I uncharacteristically challenged him on something he said. He expounded on it, and when he finished, I humorously admitted my error. Later, a few of my classmates congratulated me for my boldness.

I wondered if they would have been so quick to praise if they had known that after the class I was so shaky I rushed into an empty classroom and cried. Yet, regardless of my anxiety, this was a watershed moment in finding my voice.

Just before school ended, I received yet another insight when the words *I want life!* irrupted from the depths of my being. Everything in me was gathered up in this one passionate plea. At thirty-nine I realized there was more to life than I ever imagined. I longed for a deeper, richer, more authentic experience.

In a wrap up of the school year, each student was asked to finish the sentence: "The gift that God has given me this year has been . . ." I wrote the first thing that came to mind: *my self.* This seemed self-centered and unchristian, but I kept it and when my turn came I shared it with the rest of the class.

During that school year a path had been cleared to my in-depth self and to the God who met me there. A self who could be vulnerable and honest and courageous. Without that gift of self I could not have moved into the future that lay ahead – a future filled with uncertainty and disruption.

Chapter Eleven

By the time school ended, Paul and I were coexisting in a kind of silent truce. Underneath, a powder-keg was waiting to be ignited. In September, during an argument whose content I cannot recall, Paul lunged toward me, fists clenched. I looked at him and calmly said, "Go ahead and hit me, if that's what you want."

He backed away and walked out of the room.

I sat down and felt a shiver of fear at what could have happened. Then amazement at what did happen. The threat of being hurt had not caused me to cower, flinch or back away. Rather, a force from deep within – a power I did not know I possessed – had spontaneously stood up and squared off.

It was clear our marriage was in trouble and could not go on like this. I told Paul I wanted a separation and was afraid he would demand that I be the one to leave. After a month of tense cohabitation, Paul took the boys aside, explained what was to happen and moved into an apartment close by. Today I appreciate how honorable and difficult that was. Paul was a loving, devoted father and leaving his sons must have been gut-wrenching, although he did continue spending a lot of time with them.

Freedom can be a scary and exhilarating thing. With no outside authority — no spouse, no teacher, no religion — telling me what to do, I had to navigate through life with a different compass, with a kind of internal knowing or intuition. *I want life!* became my North Star.

I often found myself walking through the mall or on the trail at the end of my street, the one that circled a pond, with no other purpose than to take in all that I saw and heard. Patterns, colors, lights, laughter, quiet, birds, breath. Why had I not noticed these before? Life so beautiful, so vibrant, found right here, within the ordinary world, not in some mystical, spiritual world set apart.

I gradually broke away from my constant striving to be more religious. One sign of my progress became the morning I sat at Denny's counter enjoying their Grand Slam breakfast. Instead of reading the devotional booklet I had stuck in my purse, I bought a newspaper (a luxury at the time) and hungrily read it. Afterwards I noticed an absence of the guilt I usually felt when I failed to fulfill some religious obligation.

My life also expanded through a friendship. I met Linda through a twelve step growth group that met during the Sunday morning education hour and we quickly became friends. On my desk sits the memory scrapbook I assembled so that I could remember significant people, messages and photos of my new life. (At the time it seemed like something a high school girl would do but I did not let that stop me.) On the second page are two notes written by Linda. One says, "A friend is a person with whom you dare to be yourself. Thank you, friend."

Petite, with curly light brown hair, a quick smile and soft voice, Linda was genuinely warm and thoroughly unpretentious. Besides sharing honestly about ourselves in group, Linda and I had long conversations over the phone. She talked a lot about a husband who expected dinner to be ready when he came home from work, who sat sullenly in front of the TV, who hardly ever spoke. I felt bad for her and wished she could get out, yet knew her religious beliefs and financial dependency made this impossible.

One early spring afternoon Linda and I sat at her kitchen table drinking our second or third cup of coffee. Since we were on step five of our 12-Step Group – "To Admit to God, to ourselves and to another human the exact nature of our wrongs" – I decided to tell Linda about Sarah.

"Linda, there's something I need to talk about. It's the worst thing I've ever done." I tried to begin but shame took residence in my throat.

Linda suggested we relax by sitting down on the plush carpet in her living room. After a few minutes I turned to her. "This is so hard; I can't look you in the face right now."

Swiveling around, with my back toward her, I told her about my relationship with Sarah, about believing she was a misunderstood messenger from God, about doing whatever she asked of me, about being so consumed that I abandoned my family, about feeling lost and confused. When I finished I was glad she did not gasp in horror or walk away in disgust.

Linda probably said something supportive or comforting but what I remember is how quickly she started to disclose her own shame – times her husband had verbally and physically abused their young daughter while she did nothing. I listened, yet felt a little put off. I wanted to dwell in my own story a little longer. I was not yet ready to relinquish the distinction of worst sinner ever.

Linda's other note reads, "Appreciating and loving you. Thank you for 'being there,' for your time, words, prayers, care, love, friendship. You are a precious gift from God. He is so good! Thank you for being that poured out vessel fit for the Master's use."

This was obviously meant as a compliment, yet my initial reaction was to reject it. Her note was over the top, too much. I was not who she thought I was. Yet, although I could not verbalize it back then, my rejection went deeper than that.

Being a "poured out vessel fit for the Masters use" was not something I wanted to be. That kind of God did not love people, he used them. That kind of God required passive submission and unquestioning obedience. That kind of God had been played out with Sarah. Now, I was discovering a God who did ask me to give up who I was, but to become more of who I am.

Linda and I slowly drifted apart. I became frustrated with her lack of assertiveness toward her husband. I was more than disappointed when she could not leave family and religious obligations for one hour to have lunch together. As I look back now, I realize I placed too high an expectation on this one friendship and wish I could have accepted it for what it was.

Although Paul kept supporting us financially, it was not enough. I needed to find a job, yet returning to my profession was not a option. I had disqualified myself, acted unethically, broken the rules. I thought of myself as a criminal who needed to be banished.

My first job was at JC Penney's. It was humbling to have a job that required only a high school education, yet I found it challenging, especially learning to operate the cash register. I literally had nightmares about its looming, controlling presence. Unlike the scanners of today, it required manually putting in a different code for each transaction, often involving five or six steps. I didn't think I was capable of operating any machine that required more than two, so I came to work early, wrote down each step and practiced. In time I learned how to master it (or better, to cooperate with it) and felt proud of the accomplishment.

I also liked the challenge of being assigned to different departments. I enjoyed learning about the merchandise, straightening racks of clothing and home goods, greeting and assisting customers. I especially liked children's clothing and giftware. I never expected these departments could be a means of healing the little girl who still lived within, of creating a new narrative.

For example, one slow afternoon I found myself admiring a rack of little girl dresses with their pastel colors, dainty patterns and little ruffles. I held up a lavender dress with delicate, yellow flowers. As the image of a little girl wearing a crisp, new Easter dress took form, it seemed that, for just a moment, I became that pretty, innocent little girl. This was new, for I had never been, or had forgotten that I was once this pretty, this innocent. Could this basically be who I was – still?

Another morning, while dusting the figurines, I picked up a little angel with my birth month, November, written on her base. With eyes that sparkled, cheeks flushed light pink, lips curled in the gentlest of smiles, a golden halo on her blond hair and a bouquet of yellow flowers in her hands, she was altogether sweet and pure. She was my angel, my sweetness. I bought her, even though it was a luxury. When I got home I placed her on top of my dresser where she spoke to me in a language only children can hear.

One late afternoon when I was walking the mile and half home from Penney's, a wonderful feeling of satisfaction came over me. All the work for that day was finished. It was behind me, back in the store. My mind quickly contrasted this with my role as counselor, where success was nebulous and the work often clung to me long after the day had ended.

Chapter Twelve

After being separated a year, Paul broke up with his girlfriend and we began talking about getting back together. Two months later Paul's living situation fell apart and he had to move back in – now. I wasn't ready. I was afraid of losing the life I'd discovered. Paul said he could stay in the basement. I thought this would be too demeaning for him, too awkward for Aaron and Jason. We agreed he would move back in, not as boarder, but as father and husband.

As Paul was getting his things together and I was hurriedly driving home from work, I heard the words *I won't leave you* spoken within. I was surprised. Not that this reassurance was from God, but that I had been holding onto a fear that God might leave when Paul returned. Loosening my grip on the steering wheel, I took a deep breath and knew that whatever happened God was there and I would be alright.

In December of 1985, Paul moved back and I found myself hoping our marriage could be renewed – resuscitated – as I had been. At first, to help matters along, I took the role of a loving, affectionate wife. I held Paul's hand when we were walking next to each other, nestled up to him on the couch. I framed our wedding picture, displayed it on the end table next to the new portrait we had taken and hoped we could become what the images portrayed.

Yet there had been too many changes during our separation. I was not the same person. I knew I could make it without Paul. No longer focused on pleasing or appeasing him, I directed my energy on managing my own life, on being grounded, on staying in touch with my inner reality. This left Paul free to do the same. Over time, I hoped he might see something in me which led him to desire the same way of life. More likely, however, Paul saw my freedom as disconnection or even rejection.

During our separation, I had discovered the freedom to choose my own way. I now used this freedom to question domestic roles based on duty and submission. I want to believe I exercised this freedom thoughtfully and not like a rebellious teenager, that my decisions were made, not out of spite, but out of a healthy dose of self esteem.

One break from my usual behavior came during the Wisconsin State Fair. My family had already spent a day at the fair, yet there were many attractions we missed and that I wanted to see, so I asked if anyone wanted to spend another day at the fair. Disappointed to get no takers, I came up with a novel idea. I could go alone. With a new sense of power, I told Paul I was going back to the fair by myself. He objected because of the cost. I said I would take only twenty dollars with me.

I spent the day as a thirsty wanderer lapping up all the sights and sounds and smells. I reveled in the freedom to go wherever I wished, to linger over things that sparked my interest, to sit down when I was tired. My breath was taken away when I got to the top of the hill on Commonwealth Drive and encountered hundreds of people flowing together like a pulsating ocean wave. This mass of humanity, this lovely, messy mass of humanity – how I loved it!

Since then, going to the fair has become a yearly pilgrimage. A remembrance of an Independence Day. A celebration of life in excess.

There were other actions, small yet significant, that brought out my sense of liberation. One day I needed to find a blouse that would go with a particular skirt and jacket and found the perfect match. I never bought anything at full price, never even looked at anything that was not on sale. Yet, with just a brief pause to consider whether I could actually do it, I bought it at full price, a new sense of self-worth edging out any sense of guilt.

On a slow, summer day I pulled the lounge chair out in front, stretched out, and opened a novel. I had not read much fiction since college. I thought it a bit frivolous. There was always someone to attend to, some work to get done. Reading again was glorious. The story warmed my soul, the sun warmed my body. I had a repeat performance the following day, even though there was a sink full of dirty dishes beckoning me back inside.

I reconnected with my athletic self by joining our church's women's softball team. I had not played since having children, so I was delighted and a bit surprised that I still knew how to catch and hit. One evening, in the middle of the season, before falling asleep, I found myself replaying a time at bat when I hit the ball way past the infielders (or maybe just out of their reach.)

I began swimming laps at a community pool. After one of my first swims, sitting alone in the locker room, taking it all in – the bench, the lockers, the showers, the smell of chlorine, my tired muscles – I felt a kind of oneness with it all. *This is a place where I belong,* I thought. I kept track of all the laps I swam and after many months earned a t-shirt that read: *I Swam 100 Miles at Edgewood Pool*. Although it no longer fits, it still sits in the bottom of my dresser drawer.

One night, watching television with Andrew and Matthew, I felt perfectly, wonderfully content. I felt no pressure to be doing something more productive, no guilt over wasting time. I wanted nothing but to be there with them.

Things were not so good with Paul, however. As the months passed we became more estranged. We were polite, and we no longer fought, but we never touched one another. I was terribly lonely. Lying next to him in bed was painful. I ached for some kind of connection, for a simple act of kindness, for a greeting when he came home at night.

After twenty months, with no sign or hope of change, I saw our relationship going down the same path as Paul's parents. Most of the time they acted civilly, yet years of unaddressed disappointments and grievances seeped out through caustic remarks, icy silence, or hateful looks, infecting the rest of the family, who his parents claimed were the reason they stayed together.

In order to avoid an ugly confrontation, I decided the best way to tell Paul I wanted a divorce was through writing. On August 19, 1987, the day of our twentieth anniversary (I chose this date to make a point but now see how cruel it was), I handed Paul a one page letter stating I had done all I could, nothing had changed between us and I was going on with my own life.

I struggled a lot over whether this was the right thing to do. I knew all the Bible verses that prohibited divorce. Yet I also knew what I was living was not a marriage. I was afraid Paul would try to force me out and leaving my sons again was not something I could do. After ten tension-filled days, Paul moved out.

Finding an evangelical attorney helped ease my guilt. He had also struggled over whether it was morally right to help people divorce and had concluded that his job was not to judge, but to provide a decent burial for that which was dead.

I determined to fight for as much child support and alimony as I could get, and hoped this was not motivated by spite or greed. I did not want my fight directed *against* Paul (although I'm fairly certain it came across this way to him). I needed to fight *for* myself. In standing up for myself, in refusing to settle for less, I was taking back the self I gave up when I married.

Chapter Thirteen

After Paul left I reconnected with the socially out-going, humorous self I had been in high school. Back then sports had been a big part of my identity and I had even been voted most athletic girl of my class. Now, sports became a comfortable way to reclaim a part of myself.

Paul and I had been partners in a church "wolleyball" league – essentially, the game of volleyball played inside a racquetball court. The skill lay in anticipating where the ball would fall after ricocheting off the wall, then returning it over the net before it hit the floor. It had quickly become my favorite sport.

Teaming up with other partners brought out my unbridled competitiveness. After I slammed the ball at an opponent's feet, or dove for a ball that seemed out of reach I yelped and gave out high fives. After a particularly awesome shot I sometimes dropped to the floor and spun around on my back. You'd think I'd just won an Olympic medal. I did feel a little embarrassed, yet this did not shut down my exuberance.

When the season was over, we all met for a barbecue in Stan and Judy's backyard. I felt a wonderful and unusual sense of belonging. Perhaps because these people had already seen my outrageous behavior, I wasn't afraid of doing or saying something stupid. After all, I'd already made a fool of myself on the court.

I started golfing again. When I was thirteen I learned to play the game at the course just a few blocks from our home. I loved driving a long ball down the fairway, especially when people were standing around watching. Golf is what brought Dad and I together. We played without saying much. He looked away when I swore or pounded my club in the dirt after missing a shot. Occasionally Dad offered a suggestion and I actually listened. Although I never told him, being with him meant a lot to me. His calm, unhurried presence assured me that all was well.

During college breaks family members often played golf together. I most liked playing with the guys. My first 'date' with Paul was on the golf course. He'd been invited for Thanksgiving dinner by David (they were college friends) and we golfed afterwards. I beat him. Then we married. I never beat him again.

Paul bought a family membership on a nine hole course and while we were haggling over divorce issues, graciously invited me to continue using it. Matthew and Andrew had learned to play golf at an early age. Now, uncensored by a husband, I could express the exuberance I felt as I played with them. I guess I overdid it. Often, after I exclaimed how glorious the whole thing was, or raved about one of their amazing shots, or bragged about how good I was at their age, Matthew walked ahead while Andrew gave some witty remark.

Feeling guilty about not helping others, I joined a caregivers group at church. Much of our training reviewed what I already knew, at least in theory. It stressed the need to maintain a healthy degree of compassionate detachment so the helper doesn't slide into the pit with the helpee. This of course led me to think about what had happened with Sarah – about losing my self while caring about her, about taking responsibility that did not belong with me. I could see this now. Why couldn't I see it then?

After visiting one person a few times I was relieved when no one else was assigned to me. What I needed was to be the recipient of care, not the giver. Yet, like so many, asking for help was difficult. It was a sign of weakness and vulnerability. Though I did not ask, I received.

At the start of our monthly meetings, before discussing the people who were receiving care, each member talked a few minutes about their own life. I mostly shared about struggles I was having in my marriage and always felt heard and accepted, even after I announced my decision to divorce.

Carol and I were asked to attend a twelve day Stephen Ministry leadership training in Florida. Since I had limited income, the church paid for my conference fees and an elderly couple I barely knew paid for most of my airfare, a generosity I felt unworthy of. Because of this, I never thanked them adequately.

I had been outside of the midwest only one time. When I was sixteen I flew to Tucson to visit Gramma, then took a greyhound bus to see my boyfriend, who had just moved to Los Angeles. In all likelihood my parents consented to this because he was the son of a Lutheran pastor. Keith, however, did not prove to be the spanking-clean, morally upright boy they thought he was.

Now, as a forty-two year old woman, stepping off the plane in Florida was like stepping into another universe. Florida opened it's arms to me. It liberated me from the narrow boundaries that had defined my world. It introduced me to me the broader world and gave me a place in it. And I rose to the occasion. I was personable, spontaneous, humorous and brave and have photographs to prove it.

My favorite shows me standing, with arms outstretched, on an expanse of white sand, surrounded by seagulls. Moments before I had dug my feet in the soft sand and ran alongside the birds as they took flight. Wanting to remember the unmitigated joy I felt then, I asked Carol to take the picture.

Another photo is of an alligator sunning itself on the riverbank. I took the picture after urging a classmate to come with me in the rowboat "to see how close we can get." I rowed out and we got within a stone's toss of the predator. With heart pounding, I rowed even closer and took the picture. My boat-mate finally suggested we go no farther and I gratefully acquiesced.

There is a picture of Carol and me sitting in our motel room. She is seated on a chair looking at the camera. I am in profile, sitting cross legged on the end of the bed, looking at her. Our smiles are relaxed and natural. At first I felt uncomfortable sharing a motel room with her, (a Sarah fallout)? At the end of our stay, however, Carol's relaxed manner made me feel so at ease I wanted to remember the moment.

Patricia, a smartly dressed, articulate, personable woman in her mid-30s is also pictured. She was the first published author I ever met. I kept watching to see if she reveled in this status or acted superior. She never did. As my admiration for her grew, so did my desire to become a real writer. I bought her light, humorous book of instruction for parents and after reading it thought, *I can do that, probably better.* (*N*ow, having experienced how difficult it is to craft even one good sentence, let alone an entire story, I take this back.)

Chapter Fourteen

After the divorce settlement I had to find a way to earn more money. Returning to my profession was still not an option. I could not yet trust myself and was fearful of loosing my way, and my self, once again.

There were many short-term jobs: working behind the jewelry counter at Wards during the Christmas season, pitching Grundy Window and Doors in an exhibit during the Wisconsin State Fair, teaching children how to swim at the local pool.

A job in Penney's customer service department taught me the knack of multi-tasking. Besides receiving and retrieving catalogue items, wrapping gifts, processing charge payments, answering questions and resolving complaints, we answered the store phone. Eventually, I learned to attend only to the task – to the person – in front of me. When I felt harried, I tried not to let my face show it and was especially proud of this. I left thinking that if I can do this job, I can do anything.

During college I had taken a summer job as a lifeguard and at forty-three thought that I could try it again. After passing courses in CPR, first aid and advanced lifesaving (I thanked my drowning victim for going easy on me), I was a lifeguard at a beach on Long Lake (same lake, different shore, where I had felt so oppressed with Sarah's neediness.)

Being among men and women in their twenties made me feel a bit out of place, but I did not allow that to dampen my happiness. Spending every day at a lake once again (and getting paid for it!) brought me back to the carefree summer days of my childhood. I never saved anyone, but basking in the sun at Long Lake saved yet another part of me. It brought peace and vigor. I felt youthful. Life was full of possibilities.

I took a brief foray into the business world. As a temp I sorted and delivered mail in an underwriting department of a large insurance company, then was hired to enter data. What kind, I have forgotten. What it was used for, I never quite knew. Every day I asked myself if this could be the start of a new career, if somehow I could make it work, if I could begin climbing that corporate ladder. After eight months I concluded that working in a company whose goal was to deny insurance benefits by any means possible might offer me a living but would rob me of a life. I resigned.

When I look back now, I am thankful for being able to hold such a variety of jobs. Each one taught me about living an ordinary life in the real world, outside the religious enclave that had separated me from others for so long. I was unaware, however, of the effect my erratic, unstable employment was having on my children until Andrew recently disclosed how much anxiety this caused. Perhaps this instability was part of the reason why, at age sixteen, Matthew chose to live with his father.

With their low pay and sporadic hours, these jobs also helped me accept the reality that I must return to my profession to support myself and Andrew, who was now a sophomore in high school. Matthew would continue living with his father until he graduated from high school.

It had been six years since Sarah and I was not the same person. My identity was not so dependent on what I could do or be for another. I was more aware of my own needs and the importance of caring for myself as much as others. I knew, no matter how sincere or dedicated I was, I did not have the power to save anyone.

In May of 1990 I took a social work job in an agency that helped unaccompanied refugee minors. Most were Vietnamese. All needed to be under the age of eighteen, although it was commonly known that some, with forged birth records, were older.

When they arrived to America, usually after a lengthy stay in a refugee camp, they first needed to be placed in licensed foster homes. We placed them in Vietnamese homes initially, then after they learned sufficient English, either American or Vietnamese homes. We then helped them acclimate to their new country, acquire green cards and medical insurance, begin ESL classes, and enroll in school.

The staff consisted of a director, receptionist and eight social workers – four Vietnamese and four American-born (a title that honored Vietnamese who were also American citizens). Vietnamese workers, of course, communicated with youth not yet fluent in English and usually engaged in most of the conversations with Vietnamese foster parents.

Working alongside colleagues from another culture enriched my life and broadened my worldview. I tried to immerse myself in this strange culture. I wanted to learn as much as I could, as fast as I could. I watched their behavior and interactions, I listened to the cadence of their language, I asked questions. They graciously brought me into their lives, answered all my questions, taught me about their country, explained the reason behind certain odd behaviors by newly arrived youth. I admired their respectful, deferential behavior and could not help but contrast this with the rude, abrasive manners of the "ugly American."

Every foster home was assigned both a Vietnamese and American social worker. Whenever possible monthly visits (or more as needed) were scheduled so both workers could be present. Being in this kind of partnership felt much lighter and more rewarding than being a lone counselor.

In Vietnamese homes I picked up cues on how to act by observing my partner. Usually this meant being polite, smiling, sitting quietly and sipping my coffee. Nuanced, difficult topics often shifted from English to their native language, with brief interruptions to translate what was being said to me.

In American homes my role was much more active. I brought in everything I had learned about the Vietnamese culture as I tried to support and educate foster parents in a role best defined as aunt and uncle rather than mother and father, even though the youth, out of respect, called them mom and dad.

Being social was a key ingredient in this setting. The staff frequently gathered for lunch at a Vietnamese restaurant. We all attended Tet, a New Year's celebration filled with colorful banners, platters of traditional dishes, dancing dragons and blaring music in a tonal quality that I tried to enjoy but which grated on my Western ears. Tet was also the time to visit family and friends, to present small gifts and to forgive anyone who had offended you that year. A clean slate given to everyone at the start of the new year. What an idea!

Straining to understand what was being said through thick accents and trying to internalize a sense of what it meant to be Vietnamese eventually left me feeling confused and unhinged. Needing time to figure out what was going on in me, my casual outdoor strolls turned into power walks. I wondered, given all this cross-cultural learning, why I felt so disjointed.

I discovered that a clash of cultural values was at the bottom of my anxiety. My attempt to absorb another way of life disrupted long held values which had sat unexamined and undisturbed. Since values are an integral part of who we are, my sense of self had been shaken.

I tried to find words to describe what I had observed about the Vietnamese culture. Vietnamese valued family, loyalty, duty and harmony. A person's identity came out of relationships with extended family members. Based on age, position and gender, one was given a prescribed role to fulfill. This was aptly demonstrated by the reverence Vietnamese youth displayed toward their elders – including social workers and foster parents.

Americans, on the other hand, placed a high value on individual liberty and self-determination. It was personal freedom, not preservation of the family that mattered most.

All in all, the Vietnamese way rubbed hard against these American values. Wasn't acting out of a sense of duty constrictive and dishonest? Isn't the quest of discovering one's authentic self the greatest purpose in life? Which one was right? Family loyalty certainly had not played out well in my life. I had spent years carving out an identity outside the roles of daughter and wife. I had even been willing to discard the role of mother in quest of something more.

Over time I came to see that trying to determine which cultural values were right was impossible and fruitless. Somehow, I came to hold both viewpoints, and my inner turmoil subsided.

Working with people different than me also led me to embrace our common humanity. One morning I entered our building and saw the Vietnamese staff gathered at the end of the hallway socializing as usual. Instead of waving good morning and turning into my office as I usually did, I kept walking. As soon as I joined them I felt a sense of belonging and immediately recognized this as the same feeling I had experienced with my Christian friends back in Ohio. It was mind blowing to experience such a profound connection with people outside the Christian faith; yet, all I could do was receive it.

I was impressed by the humble service of Lan, a practicing Buddhist. During a staff meeting I asked if anyone could help me move and, without hesitation, Lan said he could. I knew how busy he was with raising two sons, advocating on behalf of relatives still in refugee camps and assisting so many refugees in and out of our program.

On moving day I directed and watched as Lan and his two teenage sons (along with Andrew) lifted and hauled heavy boxes and furniture in and out of a moving van. What I saw was the exorbitant, uncomplaining generosity of a man taking a half day out of his busy schedule to help a person in need. This left me wondering if my brand of Christianity showed so clearly.

For over two years questions about recently immigrated youth whirled around in my mind before I felt comfortable enough to voice them to colleagues. Finally, it felt dishonest not to. I questioned if our program was doing these newest arrivals a service by uprooting them from their families and culture, no longer because they were persecuted, but because they desired a better financial life, and believed Americas' streets were paved with gold. Were the hardships they faced in America worth all they left behind?

Lan, who had fled from his country fifteen years before, patiently informed me of things I did not know. He told me that many who still lived in the camps fled government positions and were seen as rebels by the current regime. Without programs like ours they would be forced to return to Vietnam, disgraced. In all likelihood they would face discrimination and be unable to find adequate work. With this information my doubts were relieved and my questions stopped.

The issue, however, was not settled with some of the others. Thomas, an easy-going, congenial man in his mid-thirties, held a place of esteem among the staff, which I suspected had been granted him because he had been married (and then divorced) to a Vietnamese woman. For some reason his winsome smile, sunny disposition, and unflappable calmness grated me.

Thomas and I often ate our lunch at the same time. Sitting at the table with him, I watched him meticulously spread cheese on crackers and tried to listen to another rambling story that went nowhere. Eventually I became so irritated that, instead of forcing myself to socialize, I read a magazine.

Shortly after Thomas was promoted to co-director he summoned me to his office and closed the door. I knew something was up. Thomas said Sandy (the social worker with the longest employment) had been offended by my questions. He could not tolerate that kind of rift. My questions were out of bounds and could threaten the purpose of the program, the ground on which it was built. *But I don't have that kind of power,* I thought.

I told him my questions had been answered after hearing Lan explain why Vietnamese still needed to come to America. That didn't matter. What I did was unacceptable. He couldn't allow it.

Thomas mentioned how rude it was when I read a magazine while he was sitting at the table next to me. I apologized. He said it had already been decided. When it finally sunk in, I said, "Thomas, you didn't have to do it this way."

He informed me that I was eligible for unemployment compensation.

He told me not to call any of the foster parents; he would tell them of my leave-taking. Thomas directed me to pack my things. I walked out of his office and closed the door.

Holding a small box of personal items, looking down a hallway that seemed much too long, with Thomas walking a few feet behind, I said my goodbyes to colleagues. Lucy, the most recently hired, warmly hugged me and whispered, "I understand." I thanked Kim, a Vietnamese Catholic nun, for inspiring me with her humble service. I praised Huang, the youngest Vietnamese social worker, for the natural way he connected with the youth.

Two foster parents wrote letters to Thomas that he sent on to me. Each questioned why I had left so abruptly and cited the exceptional help and support they had received from me. Their letters meant more than they will ever know. After I read them a few times, I decided not to keep them. Re-reading them could lead to bitterness, which could end up consuming me.

I did keep a note written by the previous director: "Eileen - Thank you for everything you've given me over the past year – your support, your commitment and your insight. I've appreciated the wisdom you bring to this program."

This time, there was no question of whether I'd stay in my profession. I needed the income and trusted God to guide me to the next job. I also needed a break, and decided to collect unemployment for a while.

Again, it was being in the moment, engaging in simple, solitary activities that brought me peace. I spent a lot of time in nature. I walked around the beautifully crafted lake outside my apartment complex and on the cross country path behind my sons' high school.

I stopped to consider things that caught my attention, that seemed to speak of a deeper truth. One lone leaf clinging onto a branch on a cold, blustery winter day immediately drew me to my past, to how tenaciously I had clung to life. A spring plant sprouting from the stump of an old tree trunk spoke of the force of new life pushing out from hard, unlikely places.

Chapter Fifteen

My next position was with an agency that formed contracts with the county's child protection and mental health services. I was one of four women hired for a new program that provided intensive in-home family counseling for adolescents who were acting out. Most of the families were well known to school and county officials. If the youth's behavior did not change, he or she would be facing an "out-of-home placement."

Many parents and kids felt misunderstood and judged, even harassed, by school and county officials. When we met them on their turf, when we aligned ourselves with their desires (often getting the county off their backs), they started sharing their concerns and hardships. Along with this, they shared things about themselves that were not found in any case file back in the county office.

A mother living in what was called a "garbage house" made a path through the clutter to a polished display case in the corner of the living room. In it were artfully arranged flowers, colorful glass paper weights and two Hummel figurines.

A girl who frequently skipped classes and seldom spoke pointed to the horse figurines lined up on a shelf in her bedroom. As I asked about these, she brought out her drawings and talked about how much she missed her horse.

A tough teen-age boy with a history of disruptive, defiant behavior pointed out his baseball paraphernalia. I told him I was pretty good at baseball and an outdoor game of catch became a regular part of our time together.

The families I visited lived in houses scattered throughout the county, which required long drives down winding, two lane county roads. Except during snowfalls, I enjoyed traveling these roads. The rolling fields of corn and grass nourished my soul. Analytical thoughts came to an end and a deeper place opened up, a place of rest and beauty, a place where I could calmly attend to whatever was waiting for me at the next house.

In a profession where success was uncertain, a little acknowledgment went a long way. Charlene, a poor, single mother of three, kept struggling with one thing, then another. After a year, when our time was coming to an end, she handed me a note: "Thanks for letting us know our family is worth working things out. We owe you so much." At the time, I did not realize the difference I could make by just showing up week after week.

Another note given to me read: "You did an enormous amount for us. We will be grateful always. Hoping that you will continue to gift others for a long time to come. Henry." A Catholic priest until he fell in love and married, Henry was ill-prepared to be a father to his wife's teenage son. I thought I had helped some, but his words gave me needed assurance.

I received the same acceptance and encouragement I tried to give clients from Janet, the director. Janet let me speak, to go where I needed to go. I never felt criticized or judged. She asked good questions about the families and helped me accept what it was I could realistically do. Rather than promoting the agenda of the agency, Janet promoted the staff, enabling us to become better.

During one supervisory meeting I started to choke up when talking about a fourteen-year-old girl who had been molested. Janet said, "What's going on, Eileen?"

"This is getting a little too close," I replied, then paused. I said, "I came real close to being raped in high school. Boys heard about it and started to use me. I didn't know what was happening. I was so naive."

"Oh, I'm so sorry, Eileen, so sorry this happened to you."

Her immediate, sincere expression of sympathy felt like a balm. I wanted more, but remained quiet. Janet asked if I needed to take a break.

I walked into another room and found myself doubting whether this long buried incident really was interfering with my work. Maybe I had exaggerated its effect, had brought it up to get special attention.

When I returned I felt a little uncomfortable, yet Janet did not treat me any differently. Although she had the credentials and experience, she did not slip into the role of therapist. She continued being my supervisor and directed the conversation back to the client. As I look back on this now, I can see that, at a time I felt weak and vulnerable, her unflinching regard for me as an effective helping professional was the most therapeutic thing she could have done.

Janet left the agency to stay at home with her newborn son. Debra was chosen as director. I wasn't surprised. I knew she would bring in revenue, start up new programs, keep things running smoothly. I also knew she could not be my supervisor.

Debra's flamboyant dress, quick wit and rapid speech, traits I put to her California roots, overwhelmed me. I was intimidated by her strong personality and self-assurance. I could not see myself being her subordinate. I feared being dominated, of crumbling under her influence, of being unable to defend myself. So I resigned.

When the director of county social services heard I was going to leave she handed me a note: "Thank you for your highly professional work with our clients – I especially appreciate your willingness to speak candidly about problems and resolutions as needed." I was glad at least one person appreciated my candidness.

Chapter Sixteen

If nothing else, I had become somewhat of an expert in job interviews and beat out three others for a social work position in the behavioral health unit of a general hospital. Being in a psychiatric ward was like stepping into a strange world where doctors reigned, where psycho-chemistry was the jargon, medication the goal and patient charts evidence that all was in order. A nurses' station behind an impenetrable glass wall kept two distinct classes – staff and patient – separate.

Patients entered this world after being assessed as a threat to themselves or others. First-timers were quickly transferred to a more open unit and released after their 72 hour hold expired. Those who remained on the locked unit were often repeaters, with diagnoses such as paranoid schizophrenia or bi-polar. Some had been released from a state hospital after a new community-based policy was enacted. Unable to adjust in a group home, unwilling to take medication that flat-lined emotions, they ended up living on the street, drawing unwanted attention. In the hospital they were given new medication and sent out under the auspices of an over-worked county case manager.

On the locked unit I watched as staff surrounded a defiant patient who was forced to lie down on a bed, restrained by leather straps and injected with a sedative. Whereas witnessing a child's resistance to being restrained can be disturbing, seeing an adult fight with a kind of animalistic instinct was exponentially worse. Perhaps this showed up in my face, for after being on the locked ward for only a short time, I was never asked to participate in a restraint or assigned a highly aggressive patient.

Many of the patients I saw expressed dismay about being locked in with such disturbed, unwieldy patients. They felt frightened and betrayed. Their grievances weighed heavily on me. After two months, trying to understand why I felt so down, so defeated, I made this journal entry:

> I have the familiar feeling that what I'm doing for the patients isn't enough, and that it could never be enough. Even though I'm fulfilling all job expectations and doing even more, I am still under condemnation. It's not enough. I can't give them what they need. I want to reassure them that everything will be alright, that they are alright, but nothing I say is enough. I end up giving out of compulsion, then resent the time I give. Until I have no more, and feel dried up. Yet, I still think I need to go back and give more. I want to make up for the harm this place is doing to them. I want to make it right.

As I wrote this I understood that my deepest desire – to make up for the harm this place is doing to them, to make it right – was impossible. So, I started to grind out another way of operating. I ignored the unrealistic dictates of my conscience and did only the tasks I had been assigned. This wasn't easy; it felt like a cop-out. But I also learned to live with limitations. A year later I could see the difference and wrote:

Knowing how little I can do for (some) patients here, I still am able to find the energy to just do the tasks required – and this has felt empowering. I don't need so much to be something to the patients. My expectations for what I can do/be for others are becoming much more realistic. I can just "do the job" and be okay with this, and this is new in me – this acceptance of "what is" and living within my own limitations.

One thing I never came to accept was the view that medication was the first and primary treatment method. Asserting my belief within the safety of my journal I wrote:

I don't think people should turn their mental/emotional discord over to anyone else, but especially to a physician who spends little time with them, who is looking for symptoms to fit into a diagnosis and whose primary/only way of helping is by prescribing medication. They 'take over.'

In her book *Growing Strong at Broken Places*, Paula Ripple makes the point more forcefully: "When people in counseling and other health professions cannot tolerate the presence of pain in the life of the client, they become agents of destruction rather than of growth. The promise of instant pain removal is not therapeutic in the long-distance run toward a more complete life." (Ave Maria Press, 1986, p 15)

I also struggled with the implicit expectation that staff congregate in the nurses' station for "team building." To me the atmosphere was anything but collaborative. More like the reality TV program *Survivor*, back biting was rampant, alliances were sought, any semblance of power was protected.

My experiences in the nurses station can be summed up like this: I walk into the nurses' station and quickly scan the room. Each person is in their usual place, sitting in a particular chair, standing at a certain spot, engaged in conversation. No one acknowledges me. I sit in the only vacant chair at the far end of the long counter and feel acutely, conspicuously cut off from the others. I long to take part in the conversation but stop myself from saying anything for fear of appearing too needy, too over-bearing. The longer I sit, tongue-tied, the more conspicuous I feel. *What's wrong with me? Why can't I just say something? Anything.* With my heart racing, I think, *I've gotta get outa here!* and quietly leave.

I mentioned the discomfort I felt when I was in the nurses' station to my supervisor. Margaret was one of most gregarious, confident persons I had ever met. Many of our conversations centered on the disgruntled, resentful attitude that permeated the hospital culture, what lay beneath this, and steps being taken to change it. Margaret encouraged me to keep trying to find my place in the mix: "Lighten up, just be yourself. You have a lot to offer, good insight. I know you can help change the milieu, make it more positive."

I tried, but I was not Margaret. So instead I spent time in the only other place designated for social workers – a dreary, seldom-used room upstairs lined with old desks and discarded forms. Even though I felt as much of a castaway as the desks and forms, it was better than the nurses station. I also found a small park down the street where I occasionally ate lunch, until I was reprimanded for being unavailable for a nurse's request.

Eventually I learned other ways of being in the nurses' station by watching my colleagues. John had worked with adolescents on the floor above for a number of years. Leading adolescent groups and family sessions kept him very busy so he spent little time in the nurses' station below. When he was there, his response to yet another sarcastic remark about his absence was to ignore it or respond with some humorous quip, then go on his way. I thanked John for modeling an affable way to deflect criticism. He didn't think it was anything noteworthy.

Peter, an older, well-educated man who had settled into a job beneath his abilities, would stroll into the nurses' station, move a chair beside the rack of charts, pull out a chart, cross a foot over his knee, and lean back. Then, peering over the chart, oblivious to the grimaces appearing on the faces around him, he would pontificate about some obscure subject.

I too started grabbing a chart before sitting down. It worked. Having this chart in front of me acted as a shield from imaginary or real barbs coming from others. Even if I just pretended to be engrossed, it gave me something to focus on besides my own discomfort.

Listening to staff complaints and trying to discern what was beneath them was exhausting and fruitless so I decided to focus on improving my job, to spend more time on the unit, even though this was frowned upon. A comment in my performance appraisal confirmed this: "Peer feedback would indicate that growth could be continued in the area of functioning as a team member."

The atmosphere was different on the other side of the glass wall. People seemed more genuine and honest. Some patients expressed how foolish or embarrassed they felt to be in this place. Others expressed anger. Most were experiencing a sense of bewilderment or disorientation. With pretenses stripped away, with no need to vie for position or status, many came together to help and encourage one another. Even to show kindness. All shared one common goal – to get out. As I walked back into the glass-encased nurses' station, I often felt like we were the ones who were really locked up.

Completing social assessments became not only a requirement, but time to help clients reflect on what had led to their hospitalization and how they could prevent this from happening again. For many women, the breakdown of a relationship lay behind their spiraling feelings and actions. Their significant others were often demeaning and abusive, yet many of them believed it was the best they could do. Having someone was better than being alone.

For others, a job change precipitated feelings of worthlessness, despair, and hopelessness. One poised, middle aged gentleman had recently been denied the promotion he'd been promised. We talked about other career paths, about letting go of the bitterness, and about other things he valued. Yet he never budged from the belief that without this job his life was over. After agreeing to take antidepressants and receive psychotherapy, he was released from the hospital. Our conversations, however, made me anxious about what he might do.

Besides medication, the other primary treatment option was group education. Resentment ran deep toward those who did not volunteer as much as others. Most groups centered on the patient's need to take medication and to call someone when they felt overwhelmed. These steps were helpful, yet this sole focus presented the doctor as expert, medication as the only treatment, and other people as rescuers. This could add to a client's sense of helplessness and dependency rather than to their self-efficacy.

While rifling through some workbooks I found in the old nurses' station, I came across discarded mental health handouts on topics around managing stress, finding leisure time activities, setting realistic goals and communicating more assertively. This excited me. I now had topics to bring to the group, topics that had helped me manage and change my life after my world collapsed. I believed patients could learn to do the same.

Because most patients stayed only a few days, group members changed weekly so I never knew what to expect from one meeting to the next. This caused a fair amount of anxiety. I found that deliberately taking my time while arranging the chairs before the group meeting helped settle me down. My focus centered on the feel of each chair, the sound as it was moved, the inhale and exhale of my breath. As my breathing slowed and deepened I felt my consciousness shift downward – into an inner space of calm acceptance and openness. Thanking God, I felt ready for whatever might happen.

At the start of the group everyone introduced themselves, The topic was presented and all were invited to make suggestions. To show that each comment was valued, I wrote it on the blackboard. When there was silence, I offered a few more ideas. At the end of the session, I reviewed all the comments and summarized what we had learned.

I grew more and more confident. I liked standing in front of others, encouraging them to speak out, writing down their responses, pushing for more. I was a teacher and never knew it! The positive, playful energy and synergy felt light, joyful. Like a fresh wave of the Spirit. It buoyed me up. Perhaps it did the same for the others.

My evaluator seemed to think so. On the two-year performance appraisal she wrote: "Eileen provides quality patient care both on an individual basis and in groups. She is able to establish rapport and demonstrates empathy/caring while empowering the client to identify and try more effective coping skills."

I felt even more affirmed by a note written by the newly appointed director: "Eileen has very good self-assessment skills which I believe serve her well professionally." This took me back to what I had lacked with Sarah, to the long journey that I had been on since.

Besides finding ways to perform the job that were consistent with my beliefs, I found satisfaction from my association with a doctor and a fitness center. Although psychiatrists infrequently attended the early morning staff meeting, Dr. Sponheim attended every morning and actually listened and asked questions. She even read the social assessments and consulted with nurses, therapists and social workers before making treatment plans.

After a patient defiantly refused to give her some personal information, she asked me to try. When I brought back the needed details, she marveled at my people skills while I marveled at the sense of value I felt. Dr. Shonheim continued to ask for my services and viewpoint and when I told her I'd be leaving acted genuinely disappointed. I was taken aback. In the thirty months I had been there I never thought anyone noticed or cared about how I did my job.

The hospital's physical fitness facility became my decompression center. Even though mentally exhausted, I forced myself to go. Placing my feet solidly on the treadmill, pushing my legs and arms through the weights brought me into my body and gave relief to a mind always at work, surveying the surroundings, trying to make sense of whatever was going on.

Margaret told me that by working in a clinical setting and receiving supervision from her I had already met most of the requirements to become a licensed independent clinical social worker, the highest level a master degree social worker could go. All I had to do was pass a state test. This surprised me. I had never sought, nor considered this a possibility. Yet, with nothing to lose, to prove I could do it, I took the test.

I passed, and was approved for licensure as an LICSW. My test score was 74, with the cut off score being 70. I don't know which feeling was more prominent, relief for having gotten through, excitement for having passed, or disappointment for having just barely passed.

Chapter Seventeen

Working in the psychiatric hospital felt like balancing on a tightrope with no net. Living in the country felt safe. It soothed my mind and renewed my spirit.

When Andrew was about to graduate from college and no longer needed a place to stay during the summer, I moved to a one bedroom apartment further north. The first time I drove down Forrest Street, I knew I was home.

In fact, its similarity to the place where I grew up was uncanny. My family moved to a small, rural town in northern Ohio in 1948. David was about to start kindergarten, I was almost three and Pamela was just a year and a half.

Our house, fondly called "the cottage," was at the end of a mile-long, winding dirt road bordered by fields of weeds and prairie grasses and groves of trees. Branching off from this main road were four short, dead-end streets. Our street, Qualla, was the last one. As a kid sitting in the back seat of the car on that long drive, it seemed our street was the end of the world. We could go no further.

Just past our house a fence separated our neighborhood from miles of uninhabited state land. Across the street a pond was nestled at the bottom of gently rolling hills. At the other end of Qualla lay a mucky swamp with a labyrinth of twisted limbs just below the surface where snakes and rats lived. No one ever ventured close to that dark wilderness. I didn't even like to think about it.

It is only now that I can appreciate these clear boundary markers that delineated my little world, that kept me safe. Staying within these, I never got lost or was afraid.

Trees played a prominent role in my growing years. The two tall pine trees standing on either side of the front steps of the cottage became faithful, steady sentinels, watching over my family, guarding us from all harm.

I can still picture the large oak on the corner of our street, its thick, rough bark and stately branches. A metal pump with a red handle is at its side. I am four or five years old sitting on the ground erecting dams and trenches for the water that has spilled from the pump.

I wonder how often I played in this private world of water and dirt, sticks and stones. Even though it might have been the place I went to when I felt rejected, it was also a peaceful, playful sanctuary.

When I am older I climb that tree, reaching as high as I can before perching on a thick branch. Gazing down, I marvel at how differently everything looks. The blue house on the corner, where my sometimes friend Peggy Savari (who I declared – to her face – was going to hell because she was Catholic) lives, isn't quite so massive. The house on the other side of our cottage, even smaller than ours, with the old man we never see, looks minuscule. The Burquist house down on the other side of Qualla, with its three scruffy kids whose names I can never remember, appears too close. And our cottage! It looks like a doll house.

Sitting on that branch looking down, it suddenly hits me. All of us are small – vulnerable. No one is safe. Life is precarious. This scares me. For a brief moment I find a solution. *I will rule over it all.* Almost as quickly, reality takes hold. *No, I can't, I don't have that kind of power. I am just as small, even smaller, than everyone else.* Still shaken, I carefully climb down the tree and put my feet on ground that feels solid, yet not quite.

When I first drove down Forrest Street 50 years later, the first thing I noticed was a tall grove of evergreens. This was followed by trees I later learned were ash, red oak, aspen, hickory and birch, easily recognized by its stunning white bark. A few houses sat back from the road and a farmer's fallow field lined the horizon on the other side of the road.

Following the directions I'd been given, I drove to the end of the road and pulled into the driveway just past the huge spruce tree. The owners, Ken and Dottie, a middle aged couple with no children, warmly greeted me.

We sat down at the kitchen table and after getting acquainted walked to the back of their house and entered a newly refurbished basement, complete with living room, kitchen, small bedroom and bathroom. As they detailed Ken's wall construction and built-in bookcases and Dottie's eye for interior design, the care and pride they took in this project became obvious.

But there was more. A small pond, with a grove of small birch trees, lay in the backyard. This cinched it. I signed a one-year lease and stayed for five.

I was glad the place had no second bedroom, glad it would not be possible for anyone else to live there. For the first time in my life I would live entirely alone, responsible for caring only for my self. To honor this self, I put up the diplomas and certificates I had earned over the years instead of the family pictures that had hung on a wall for some twenty years.

What I recall most vividly from this time is slowly walking down that half mile road. I never hurried. Breathing in the quiet, resting in the solitude, I was filled with peace. I wanted nothing but to be there. Looking at my feet stepping on a gravel road brought me to something familiar, unnamed, an ancient memory. *I am here. This is me. These feet, this dirt road – this is me.*

I lingered over lush yellow flowers growing beside a stream of water and early ferns slowly uncurling from their center outward. No longer afraid to be alone outdoors at night, I took evening walks. With no house or street lights to dim the night sky I gazed at a myriad of stars I had never really seen before. Feeling overwhelmed and small brought me to Psalm 8:

> When I look at your heavens, the work of your fingers,
>   the moon and the stars that you have established;
>   what are human beings that you are mindful of them,
>   mortals that you care for them?

I bought a bicycle with a camera attachment, rode down country roads and took pictures of cows and horses, vast fields of soybeans, corn stalks in neat rows, old barns, rolls of hay scattered randomly on barren fields, and narrow roads leading to abandoned farmhouses.

My sense of smell became more heightened. Walking by a freshly plowed field, I picked up a clump of dark soil and inhaled its pungent odor. Tears came as I sensed the deep, hidden richness of this basic element of earth.

Home after a long, tiring day of attending to others, I broke off a small pine branch, rubbed it between my hands, inhaled deeply, and felt a deep, calming sense of being in relationship with myself return.

Living in the landscape of my childhood was calming, yet I also yearned for a little adventure. I drove up to the North Shores of Lake Superior, stopping at iconic places like Gooseberry Falls, Split Rock Lighthouse and Palisade Head.

Each trip took me further north. On top of a ridge in Grand Marais, gazing at a span of endless water on one horizon and mountain vistas on the other, I laughed, stretched out my arms, wept, ached. I longed to take it in and felt frustrated when the smallness of my being could not contain it all.

Determined to get a photograph of the rising sun over Artist's Point, I stumbled out of bed when the alarm clock went off at 5:00, hurriedly dressed, walked to the point, and sat down just as the sun was making its first glowing appearance. I waited and waited for the sun to present its full self, and when it did, I was ready.

After the roll of film was developed I gasped with delight at one photo. The sun's rays, softened behind low lying clouds, formed a golden, shimmering path through the dark waters. I had it enlarged to an eight by ten and titled it *Guiding Light*. It was the first, although not the last, photo to hang on my wall.

Hoping to draw others into the glory of creation, I affixed photos to mail order greeting cards with sayings such as Celebrate Life, All Which We Behold is Full of Blessings, Nature is the Art of God, A Thing of Beauty is a Joy Forever. Six cards bundled together with colorful ribbon became family Christmas gifts.

I displayed a rack of greeting cards and four enlarged, framed photos at an arts and crafts store. This felt risky. Would I be accepted? Would people buy my creative expressions? I was pleasantly surprised when everything but a few cards and one picture sold.

Chapter Eighteen

When Dad was seventy-one he suffered a major stroke that left him partially paralyzed and emotionally labile. Looking back, it was this tragedy that brought our fragmented family together (not only had David, Pam and I moved away from our parents, we had also pursued different religious paths). Dad's stroke also revealed family dynamics that had been hidden, yet known, to me.

We often marveled at Mom's unrelenting determination and stamina during those hard years. Attending to her husband gave her life purpose and brought out a kind of radiance and vitality we had never seen before. Dad had always been the rock of the family who took care of, protected and sheltered mom. With the often repeated refrain, "don't you kids upset your mother," he had taught us to do the same. It was now Mom's turn to take care of him.

Three years later, on my forty-eighth birthday, I was at my parents' home as a relief care-giver. As we sat at the table finishing our dinner a subject (sadly, I cannot recall what this was) came up that I knew not to pursue because it could cause a rift. This time, however, curious to know more, I asked one more question. Dad immediately spewed, "This is just like you, causing problems, digging up dirt. You've always been a troublemaker!" He slammed his fists on the table and yelled, "Get out of my house!"

I was stunned by such a raw display of emotion. His accusations hurt. I felt like a defenseless little girl. With a concentrated effort not to show how shaky I felt, I pushed my chair away from the table, stood up, and slowly walked away.

Outside, I quickly assessed my internal state and decided I was able to drive. I got in the car, took a few deep breaths and thought *maybe I'll just keep driving, never go back, that'll teach them.* I resisted an urge to gun the accelerator and carefully drove to the VFW hill a few miles away. I parked in the back of the building and let the feelings flow. Anger. Disbelief. *I can't believe what he did, my dad actually did it. Kicked me out! How could he?*

Then, a strange sense of calm, and relief, came over me as I recognized that what I had always known had finally been spoken, aloud, by my Dad. I had not conjured it up. It was not a figment of my imagination. It was based in reality. *Troublemaker. A Problem.* My place in the family, the role given to me as a child, the role I had played so well as a teen-ager. It had taken years to find another identity, yet this one was still lurking about.

I turned my thoughts to dad, wheelchair bound, living in a kind of trance-like acceptance. His blow-up wouldn't have happened had he not been left emotionally labile by the stroke. Yet his accusations coincided so well with my childhood experiences, I remained convinced this rancor had been festering underground for a very long time.

I considered taking a leisurely drive around the countryside but decided I had been gone long enough. Not wanting to cause any more trouble or worry, I drove back. Mom warmly greeted me with, "Are you ready for a piece of birthday cake?"

"In a minute. How's dad doing, you know, after the blow up?"

"I don't know what you're talking about," she replied. This was almost as shocking as dad's outburst.

I walked over to my father, knelt by the foot of his wheelchair and said, "I'm sorry I upset you. I don't want to do that. It won't happen again."

Dad looked down at the floor and said nothing (perhaps he was too embarrassed). I stood up, walked to the table and joined mom for a piece of cake washed down with lots of milk.

I now look to what little I know of dad's early life to find what might have been underneath his explosion. Dad was an only child. His dad died when he was seven. His mother worked as a domestic, cooking and cleaning for wealthy families in Toledo. Sometimes he was allowed to board in the home with her, helping in the kitchen. Sometimes he lived elsewhere (I never knew where). I imagine he was a lonely, perhaps anxious child with no real sense of home. Having a peaceful, stable family of his own meant everything.

As a rambunctious, sometimes unruly child, then rebellious adolescent, my behavior threatened his image of a secure, happy family, the place he received identity and worth. My probing question at the kitchen table did the same, only this time he couldn't suppress his anger.

One early childhood experience of being – really being – with my father stands out. Sometimes in early evening we would trek to Eagle Lake, barefoot, towels draped over our shoulders. It seemed like a long walk, but that didn't matter. I was next to Dad (David and Pam were likely there, but my memory does not include them), skipping to keep up with his long strides, looking down on the dirt path, staring at the course hair that sprouted out of his long, bony toes.

When we finally arrived at the lake I would immediately ditch my towel, scamper out on the dock, jump (or dive, when I was a older) in the water and yell "Watch me! Watch what I can do!" then perform the newest stroke while Dad patiently watched from shore. Although in the typical male Finnish language he said nothing, sometimes the corners of his mouth turned up slightly. Occasionally his head nodded approvingly.

After a while Dad would swim between the docks. How I loved to watch him. In rhythmic cadence his long, lean arms would gracefully reach out in front, again and again, while his legs easily kicked in accompaniment. I was memorized. Awestruck. Proud. In a way I could not name or explain, I knew this was my Father, yet so much of him was hidden and so, so beautiful.

I wanted more of Dad's attention. There were many things that might have prevented him from being present more often. As a taxi driver, then parole officer, Dad was finding his way in the world. Both jobs required a knack for dealing with difficult people. After a long, congested commute, I'm sure Dad was emotionally spent when he returned home, just before dinner.

I'm not sure when Dad began to drink too much, but I'm sure this took him away from us also. (This and finances were the only things my parents argued about, with Dad's drinking being the most contentious). With what was left, he didn't have enough to give a fragile wife who leaned heavily on him and three small children who clamored for his attention. Yet, Dad came home every night. I depended on this. I needed his steady, calm presence and he never let me down.

Dad was able to live at home six years after his stroke. When mom's health became compromised it was apparent that both she and Dad needed more care. A nursing home for Dad and an assisted living apartment for Mom were found close to David's home in Virginia. Mom spent every day at the nursing home. Dad became weaker. After a year, it didn't look like he would live much longer.

There is an oft-repeated family story of Mom sitting in the baseball stands, next to a woman who repeatedly yells "you done good, Donny, you done good!" whenever her son made a decent play. This expression became a way we complimented each other without getting all mushy.

One day while visiting Dad I sensed this would be the last time. We didn't talk much. After tying his shoes I looked into his face to say goodbye. Our foreheads lightly touched and Dad said "You done good, Anne, you done good." I held back the tears and quietly left. Dad died three months later.

My family and some of the nursing home staff gathered in Virginia for a memorial service. David, Pam and I each reflected on our impressions and remembrances. I spoke of Dad's quiet, steady presence, of feeling that everything was put right when he came home from work, of how significant his work came to be as I watched him finish some important paper work in the car before coming inside, or heard him firmly direct a parolee over the phone. I wondered if this had influenced my own career path.

I spoke about how Dad had the final word. When he said "that's enough!" after Pam and I spent too long in bed being silly, we stopped. I never knew what would happen if we didn't, and I never wanted to find out.

I talked about wanting to impress Dad on the golf course, about the tension between us when I was a teenager, about Dad buying and servicing a used car and gifting me with the thing I most desperately needed after my divorce.

Andrew was chosen to speak on behalf of the nine grandchildren and told stories of Grandpa reading *The Night Before Christmas* in a Finnish accent, of being his sidekick in search of a runaway cougar, of watching for inclement weather atop the VFW hill, of sliding down the hill on the fifth fairway with Grandpa in the rear. We all laughed and shared stories into the night and every so often someone mentioned how pleased Dad would be with it all.

Chapter Nineteen

It was being in a relationship with a nun that brought up painful memories around my mother. Sister Bernice's resemblance to my mother was uncanny – her small stature, the way her shoulders slouched, a certain pensive expression. One day as she stood with her back toward me, I felt terribly rejected. Since she was not a person to reject anyone, I knew my reaction, triggered by her, had come out of my past.

Sister Bernice questioned many of the practices and beliefs of her Catholic Church but, unlike many of her colleagues, chose to remain. Her true vocation came from a humanistic psychology school of education that helped people experience their in-depth selves as well as their painful pasts. After years of self-exploration and healing, she became one of its educators.

When I was forty-six I attended a workshop titled *Who Am I?* led by Bernice. Its aim was to help the eleven of us discover our authentic selves by exploring self-image, crucial choices made, undertakings that called forth the best self, acts that came naturally, people who had the greatest impact, inner resources relied upon after severe trials, and unfulfilled aspirations.

I relished the unhurried time to reflect and write around focus questions. When it came time for each of us to read our responses I became anxious, but refusing this step was not an option so I raised my voice and eventually became accustomed to the sound of it. Even so, sometimes when reading a particularly lengthy response, another voice began humming in the background. *I'm taking up way too much time. My going on and on is boring, it's taking away from someone else.* The hum receded after I finished and began listening to Bernice's thoughtful, validating comments.

I had a strong desire to keep growing in my capacity to live authentically so I went to follow-up evening sessions and attended more workshops. I watched Bernice for any signs of duplicity or pretense and when I found her to be genuinely kind and caring, someone I could trust, I began individual sessions.

Bernice never considered herself a therapist. Her title was "accompanist." She clarified this role through a letter. In response to my comments about her she wrote: "It's not quite true to say I'm not affected by you. I do feel for you, and I try to listen deeply, to hear beyond your words. What is not affected is my effort to remain grounded in myself, and not think I am going to 'fix' you, to solve your problems. I do my best to help you enter truthfully and deeply into your own experience, to understand yourself better, and to find your own solutions."

In our sessions both us were aware that I was projecting feelings I experienced with my mother onto her. Bernice encouraged me to express whatever I was feeling in the moment. In one of our first sessions I told her I felt too big, that I was scared I might bowl her over. She assured me that I would not. She could take care of herself.

Knowing it was her face that immediately brought up old, painful memories, I asked if it would be okay if I just looked at her. Bernice agreed. As I fixed my gaze on her face, especially on her eyes, I began to feel attacked, like darts were being flung at me. My stomach tightened and my body coiled. This was disconcerting as it was so similar to what I had experienced with Sarah. Yet the exercises I had done in the group sessions helped me trust my bodily sensations (with psychological content) so that I might get to their origins.

There were more sessions where sitting close to Bernice, being quiet, and focusing within, brought on these contractions. Trying to express what was going on in me came slowly. Finally I blurted out, "I can't breathe! Not enough air. There's no space for me here."

On Labor Day I felt a need to call Bernice (the reason has escaped me). Afterwards, I felt a sense of anguish over taking up her time, so I went for a long walk. When I returned home I picked up my journal and wrote:

> Sometimes it's alright to take up someone's time and attention. Others do it to me, and that's okay. I can do it too, and that's alright. Bernice can take care of herself and her own needs. I am not there to make sure I don't ask too much, to fear she'll come apart. Right now she is here for me – she is competent and qualified to be with me – to accompany me – at this time of healing. She *can* take care of herself. I need not fear that I'll bowl her over or make her incapacitated. Bernice *will* get her needs met. I don't have to take care of her like I did with Mom.

In another session, I had an inkling I should take a submissive role by kneeling at her feet. (Unlike the time I sat at Beverly's feet as a devote, this time I was intentionally taking on a role that could open me to my childhood self.) Bernice said she was okay with that. I knelt and immediately felt awkward and foolish. Bernice remained quietly seated. I breathed. My stomach spasmed, hard. I searched for words to describe what was going on. "I'm afraid to open up to you. Afraid I'll get hurt." Then, feeling terrified, I spilled out, "Please don't send me away, please don't send me away. I'll be good."

I remained dubious about whether these experiences that seemed to fly out of the past were real. Maybe, like Sarah, I was making all of it up, being overly dramatic, making a spectacle of myself to gain attention or favor. On the other hand, the way my body tightened up could offer a needed explanation of other times this had occurred.

As I examine these situations, I find certain similarities: Sarah, Mary and Bernice were all women I trusted enough to let down my defenses, to become vulnerable. As a passive observer I was keenly aware – sensitive, curious – of everything going on within and around me. Holding this duel focus within a setting I could not leave, or chose not to leave, my stomach spasmed, my body stiffened.

A reasonable explanation could then be that these bodily reactions were a defense against some kind of unconscious danger. A warning that screamed, "Watch Out! Too Close. Back away!" My contortions were not demons that had invaded my body, but a protective system within my body. I like this version of the truth. It focuses on the complex interconnectedness of the human person, God's very good creation.

Through my relationship with Bernice I learned even more about my relationship with my mother. Before one of our sessions I tried to get in touch with my feelings and wrote:

> Most of the time I look at you as larger-than-life. That's because you are still like a mother to me. I love you, Bernice. I love your patience, how unhurried I feel with you. I can take all the time I need. You don't push me to speed up or to "get on with it" as Mom did. You are just *there* with me and this is such a precious thing. I have never experienced this like I do with you. I just need you so much! These needs are very present to me now – I am open to them – they seem to come gushing out. I <u>*scream*</u> to be heard: I NEED YOU! I NEED YOU TO LOVE ME! TO RECEIVE ME. TO TAKE ME IN.

This plea was clearly an expression of my inner child's unmet, buried need. Even though I had learned that this deficiency need could never be filled, for one brief moment I experienced the bond I so desired with my mother. Wanting to capture this more fully I wrote:

> [Bernice] stands beside me – at the workshop – as I sit with my head comfortably resting on the chair – and she – standing – beside me with her arm on the chair. What peace! How safe and secure I felt. I never wanted to leave. I just wanted to be quiet, and soak in her presence. How wonderfully at peace I felt. I never wanted this moment to end.

As soon as I finished this sentence, I felt myself drop to a deeper level. To depict this descent in consciousness I drew two descending arrows with the words *I missed having a mother* at the bottom. Suddenly I was gasping for air, suffocating. I bent over, my thighs tightened. It was as if my body could not take in the shock of this devastating truth. I missed having a mother. But there was more.

One day, while I was calmly washing dishes at the kitchen sink, the words, *I am a Mistake,* rose to the surface. My body recoiled, as though I'd been shot, and I slumped to the floor. I cried. I wrapped my arms around my knees, comforting that little girl who had lived out of such an awful, mistaken belief.

As I read through more of my journal entries I am surprised at how often I needed to find words for the new realities I was experiencing with Bernice. One of the later notes reads:

> The time and space I have with Bernice are *mine* and they are given to me by Bernice, to use in whatever way I choose. This large space is mine. I am not taking up anyone else's space. I'm not taking what is not mine. And – I'm not responsible for Bernice's feelings. If she feels down or upset by anything I say, she can take care of this after our session. I need not worry about her or feel I'm responsible for making her feel better.

There came a time when I no longer felt the need to continue seeing (or paying) Bernice for individual sessions. It was both sad and liberating to leave, yet nothing had been wasted. Every risk I had taken to stay present to whatever was going on in me, to express my needs, to uncover and speak my truth had prepared me for the most challenging time of my life.

Chapter Twenty

When I was fifty-two, I became the one responsible for Mom's care. After Dad died I flew to Virginia a few times to help care for Mom, who seemed to be slipping into a depression. During our time together she revealed a reflective, insightful self I had not seen before.

Mom asked me, "Do you see me as a sissy? Am I always a baby?"

I replied, "I dunno, maybe, maybe that's just who you are. How do you see yourself?"

"Adequate. I always rise to the occasion."

Mom said Dad's death was the hardest thing she'd had to adjust to. She had never felt so lonely. She worried about how long she'd be able to do this.

One afternoon she looked at me and exclaimed, "You mean you came here just for me? All that way, for all this time?"

And later: "I don't know what I'd do if you weren't here. I don't think I'd make it." She paused and added, "But God always provides."

There were also times I felt annoyed and manipulated by her helplessness and responded curtly to her requests for help. This made it worse, so I turned to my counselor-self and tried to see things from a different perspective. I wrote:

> She experienced love from Dad when he told her to lie down when she was tired. I need to show her love in this way also. It's the only thing that can help her do for herself. Except I can't expect this from her – it can't be a manipulative thing, i.e.. I'm nice to you and do things for you in order to get you moving. I also need to tell her when I can't do something and sometimes not respond when I think she can do for herself.

To remember little moments that showed some sign of hope, I again picked up my journal and wrote:

> Signs of coming out of depression: Mom was noticing for the first time pictures in the dining room, the healthy green plant in her room, tasting food again, saying, "it's good, everything looks different when you're sick."

After seeing how well Mom did with me, David thought she would be better off living close to me. I wasn't so sure. The responsibility felt huge. Her neediness could be overwhelming. I was afraid of losing my freedom, my independence, my sense of self. Yet, David and Pam had each played an active role in caring for our parents. Now it was my turn.

Back in Wisconsin, after praying for guidance, I quickly got to work and found an assisted living apartment close by, yet not too close. After an anxious, restless night with a mind that wouldn't shut off because of all I needed to do to furnish this apartment, I picked up my journal and wrote:

> I want to please her, yet I can't take away her pain or create a perfect world for her. I will never be able to be/do what

it is you want me to be/do. I realize how much pressure I put on myself around finding a comfortable chair and bed that would keep you out of a nursing home. I can't fix you.

Tears came. I paused, letting them flow. I continued:

I can't keep you out of a nursing home if that is what you need. It this happens, it won't be my failure. I can't save you from all pain.

As this truth sunk in, I felt a deep sense of sorrow, then relief.

The next day as I continued furniture shopping my imagination began to tenderly cradle my mother as if she were a fragile child. Holding onto this image I finally relaxed and found a store with simply crafted wood furniture. I bought a twin bed with a soft mattress, a comfortable recliner, a small chest-of drawers, two end tables and a small dining room table with two chairs. I added a colorful quilt, two lamps and a blue framed picture of a golden sky, lighthouse and birds in flight with the caption: "Here with each new sunrise, life begins anew."

With her living environment and my interior environment settled, I felt as prepared as I could be. Mom arrived on January 12th, 1998, just shy of her seventy-sixth birthday. As she looked around her room she said, "Oh Eileen, everything looks so comfortable and cozy!" Grateful for her gratitude, I knew we were off to a good start and felt a spark of hope that she might be happy here.

Mom quickly adjusted to the many caregivers coming in her room, to meals eaten at a certain table in the dining room, to her recliner, to afternoon naps, to group activities. I quickly saw the need for clear boundaries.

There were times Mom tried to influence me by subtly putting me down or acting helpless. It felt like being sucked into something like a powerful vacuum cleaner. Somehow I knew that my best defense was no defense. I did not try to defend myself, argue, or acquiesce. I did not retreat or leave. Standing in the rock of my being, I remained connected with my self and with her.

When Mom's attempts to draw me in were more overt, I set firm boundaries. "No, they will not allow us to bring a cot for me to sleep beside you. No, I won't be spending the night in the nice guest room down the hall. I'm sorry, I can't come back tomorrow, I'll see you next week. Do you know you left sixteen messages on my answering machine? Stop doing that! I might not return your message right away, but I will always get back to you."

There were other hurdles to overcome, including the lackadaisical, distracted way Mom walked, or didn't walk. Whenever we were trying to get somewhere, Mom slowed down while I marched resolutely ahead. When I turned around she'd stop and smile. "Come on Mom, could you move a little faster? Look how far you've fallen behind! Just put one foot in front of the other. Hup, two, three, four. Think about walking, nothing else."

When it finally dawned on me that there was nothing I could do or say to change her, I changed. Walking toward her I gently held onto her arm and side-by-side we slowly propelled ourselves forward.

I struggled with how often to see her. I didn't want to feel overburdened or resentful. Mom would pick this up. I wanted to attend to her as I had learned to attend to others – out of inner resources gained through solitude. I decided I could handle visiting her once or twice a week. Even so, there were times I felt guilty. I thought, *I should be doing more.* Or, *I'm selfish and self-centered.*

The friendly, open way Mom approached everyone, especially those I judged as uncommunicative, never ceased to amaze me. While sitting at a table in the dining room she often turned to some vacant-eyed, mute resident, leaned forward, smiled, and asked how they were doing. Usually the person's face brightened as she or he replied.

The staff spoke highly of her: "Your mother is so outgoing, she has such a quick wit. Always a sunny disposition. She loves music, knows every song in the name-that-tune game." I was glad to hear this yet could not quite believe it. Except for the music part, this was not the person I knew.

What had stood out to me was her sullen expression and the way she stayed in the background, comfortably living in the shadow of her husband.

Perhaps it was my growing ability to be authentic with Mom that helped her speak honestly with me. Her candid disclosures became her greatest gifts to me. They revealed things I'd never imagined or only suspected. They filled in gaps of her life story and in so doing filled mine as well.

One day Mom candidly said, "You know, I'm attached to food, comfort and having company." I could see that all these needs were met in assisted living and that she seemed genuinely happy. I also saw that when these needs were disturbed, she took it personally and blamed whatever/whoever had caused the disturbance.

During a physical exam the nurse pumped up the blood pressure cuff unusually tight and I happened to catch the contorted expression on Mom's face. As soon as the nurse left the room she turned to me and said, "Why did she want to hurt me so much? I didn't do anything to her!"

A fly was buzzing around her head, annoying her greatly, and she spoke as if the fly was intentionally seeking her out, trying to irritate her. When I asked if she really thought the fly was out to get her, she showed no sign of recognizing the absurdity of such a notion.

When I look back on my mother's life, I think the roughest time for her, other than losing her husband, was being home alone with three rambunctious, puzzling preschool children who upset her need for physical comfort and adult company. I think Mom did the only thing she could to survive. She shut down. Perhaps her expressed apathy was not a rejection of me as I had always thought, but a sign of depression.

During a lull in our conversation Mom often asked where Dad was. "Is he in the room next door?" I tried different ways of gently reminding her that he was no longer with us. He died. Remember the memorial service? Mom would then frantically search her memory, acknowledge, "oh, yes, now I remember," then clutch her stomach in shock and pain as if hearing it for the first time.

After it became clear that reminding her that he was dead did not bring closure, when she asked where he was I told her he was in the next room. Mom would then nod her head knowingly and smile.

Certainly, forgetting her husband had died was a sign of dementia. But to me, her forgetfulness also signified the life she had found with him and the unbearable absurdity of existing without him. In her world he continued to live, just out of sight, in the next room.

One day Mom casually mentioned she could make herself look a certain way to illicit sympathy and help. I asked her to show me. Immediately her shoulders slumped, her eyes dropped, her mouth drooped. The look was of weary sadness, a kind of pleading helplessness. *That's it!* I thought. *That's the face I saw as a child. All these years I thought it was because of me, that I was a burden, too much for her.*

As a child I thought I was in the way so I stayed away. Mom might have taken this as rejection, for as we talked about some of our shared past, she turned to me and declared, "I think you liked Grandma more than me."

I replied, "No, that's not true. You were my mother, my only mother. How could I think more of Grandma than I did of you? I loved you!"

What I didn't say was that I never felt close to Gramma, that I felt handed off to her, that I never wanted to be her favorite. It made me feel different, guilty. I knew Mom was at odds with her mother and if her mother liked me most of all, whose side did that put me on?

A few months later Mom said, "I think Georgia's mother was more important to you than me," then paused to add, "More of a mother than I was."

I'm sure I also denied this but cannot recall what I said. This may be because I knew she was partly right. My best friend's mother was loud and dramatic. She drove Georgia crazy. Whenever we were caught skipping school or smoking, she became livid, spilling her tirade over both Georgia and me. This was scary, yet also felt strangely good, like she really cared about me. Unlike my mother's sullen expression, her anger was something I understood, something that passed.

When she first moved into her new apartment Mom told me she needed a live-in nurse. As I spend time considering what I know about her past, I think what she really longed for was a mother, the same thing I had sought throughout my life.

My mother was an only child and lived much of her childhood in her parent's boarding house in Toledo, Ohio. Uncles were the primary boarders and I imagine they doted on her, their only niece. Summers were spent on a farm with relatives in rural, central Ohio.

Mom described her mother, Elsa, as a vain woman who posed prettily for pictures, flirted with men and was the belle of Saturday night dances. Acting more like a sister than a mother, Elsa told her about personal problems and marital grievances while lying next to her in bed. Although she spent months in Arizona to relieve her asthma, Mom never mentioned missing her.

A family tragedy that was never forgotten yet seldom spoken about was the day Elsa's mother and younger, adolescent sister were found dead on the kitchen floor, asphyxiated by gasses leaking out of the oven door. There was brief speculation about a double suicide. If it was suicide, current psychological knowledge would suggest sexual abuse as the motive, with the victim likely being the adolescent girl and the perpetrator her father, my great grandfather.

This man, Oskar, Elsa's father, my mother's grandfather, was a barrel chested, white haired, staunch individualist. In a number of family photos it is his proud, aristocratic form and straightforward gaze that occupies the center of the picture.

Toward the end of her life, after Mom had been forthright with so many of her feelings, I finally asked her "What was Oskar like?"

"Well, he had a commanding presence. When he came into a room, everyone knew it. He seemed to take up all the space. He had strong opinions about a lot of things. And he could be stern. Uncompromising. Demanded things go his way. Sometimes I was afraid of him."

"Did he ever hurt you?" I softly asked.

Mom looked down and a foreboding, fierce expression washed over her face. I immediately recognized this as the face that had lodged into my child's mind, a face that had driven me away from her. But this time it was not directed at me. It went far back into a family who knew how to keep its secrets.

Mom took pride in the fact "there's never been anything so bad that I couldn't forget it." Yet bad things never really go away. While napping, Mom often fidgeted and moaned. One day after she woke up I asked what she'd been dreaming. Mom vaguely spoke about a war, about not being fed, about all the people looking for a bed. It was startling to know she may have experienced a time when she did not feel safe, have enough food or a stable place to live – basic necessities of life. I wanted to know more, but Mom would not elaborate or could not remember and it was all in the past anyway.

One early morning, after she'd lived in her assisted living apartment for a year and a half, Mom was found sitting in the shower with feces smeared around the stall, apparently delusional. Steps were immediately taken to move her to the nursing care floor. No one, including myself, questioned this decision.

Her living space now consisted of a bed, an end-table, a chair and a TV. A curtain divided her space from the resident next to her and, although I never heard her roommate speak, I think her presence was a comfort. Mom never complained about the move or her small quarters. She told me she liked her motel room with its comfortable bed, room service, pleasant staff and TV. Mom always found a way to adapt to her situation.

Although her short term memory was failing, one thing she never forgot was that one of her grandchildren – "Oh, yes Matthew!" – was soon to be married. I worried that she was too frail to attend, that the activity would be too much for her. My sister never doubted. She promised to help get her ready. She and her husband would transport her there and leave whenever Mom wanted.

Mom looked simply regal as Andrew took her arm and slowly walked her down the aisle, seating her in the front pew. At the reception she was greeted by strangers and doted on by her grandchildren. Mom took to her role as family matriarch like she'd been born for it. Even the loud music and whirling dancers did not disrupt her composure. She stayed to the very end. Pam and I marveled at a stamina we had not seen since Dad came home after his stroke.

For weeks afterwards Mom asked if there was any family event coming up. All I could say was, "No, I'm sorry Mom, nothing has been planned."

Mom became more lethargic and weak. Every exertion seemed to tire her. She vomited blood. She slept a lot. During a visit she drifted into sleep and instead of waking her up, I took a long look at her. *Such peace. This seems like her natural state of being now.* As I walked away, I found myself wishing she could stay in this peaceful place, in this rest she so relished.

A few days later I tearfully prayed, *God, please take her home. She's been with us long enough. She doesn't have anything to live for anymore. She needs to be with her husband.* Then, thinking I had stepped too far, become impertinent, added: *If this is Your will, please, please God, take her.*

Three days later, at 8:30 AM on December 4,1999, I received the phone call. "Oh no, what should I do now? What do I need to do?"

The nurse suggested that, if I wanted, I could come see the body. I did not hesitate, "Yes, yes, I'll be there shortly."

After hanging up my legs began to shake. I sat down and thought, *Slow down, breathe, this is an important time. I don't want to blow it, to miss any of it.* As my racing mind settled down the next steps became clear.

First, I called my brother and sister and told them Mom had died quietly in her sleep. Then I called my sons. Matthew agreed to come to the nursing home with me and while he drove to my house, I showered. In the car ride not much was said. I liked the quiet. It helped prepare me for whatever was to come.

A nurse opened the door to my mother's room. I saw her lying on a neatly made bed with a quilt pulled up to her chin. The door closed. I slowly walked toward her. I looked directly at her face and immediately noticed all the changes. The eyes were sunken, the chin had receded, the mouth was open. Everything had caved in. There was no life left. It was only a body. Still, I needed to touch her, to make some kind of connection. I put my hand to her face, felt the coldness and quickly pulled away. I gently laid my head on her chest.

Suddenly I heard a shrill, loud wail, like that of a mortally wounded animal and realized it had come out of me. Concerned this had disturbed others, I looked at Matthew, who was calmly standing against the wall on the other side of the room. Seeing him assured me that if I became lost in some dark, unknown emotional terrain he would bring me back.

    I turned to Mom. As I put my arms around her waist an eruption of long buried feelings spilled out and I shamelessly wept. Trying to find words to express what I was feeling, all I could say was, "I love you Mom, I love you, I've always loved you. I'm sorry Mom. I love you."

Chapter Twenty-One

My view of the Christian life continued to evolve. After being shown there are four sources of Christian truth, I realized I had relied heavily on *personal experience* and *divine revelation*. Yet, in order for the stool not to topple over, *reason* and *tradition* were needed. So, I turned to ones I had been taught to distrust and fear – those who used their intellect – scholars – for help.

The first book I read was given to me by Andrew. *To Pray and to Love*, by Roberta Bondi, a Professor of Church History, delved into the ancient monastic movement of men and women seeking to grow in love of God and neighbor through solitude and silence.

I had never before nor have I since read a book that impacted me so deeply. Bondi wrote about the human ability to have "religious experience" that did not, in fact, come from God. Having such an experience "would encourage the monk to believe that God had set her apart for special revelation so that she was both superior to and no longer in need of the rest of the community." (Augsburg Fortress, 1991, p 70)

Yes, I thought, *I once knew that terrain well. It is very dangerous.*

The monastics contended that no matter how powerful an experience is, God is not an experience. No one needs to have a religious experience in order to have a real relationship with God. They believed that what is most needed is to live in an ordinary, everyday, even routine way with God.

This simple, clear teaching shattered my distorted view that religious experience was the litmus test of a true Christian, that warm, ecstatic feelings mattered more than anything else.

In my journal, next to the Bondi excerpts I wrote, *A New Way for Me* and circled it with sun rays. I also sat down with my Bible, which I hadn't opened for years, and began reading the Psalms as Bondi suggested. I was drawn to Psalms of Lament, to writers who questioned God, who minced no words in expressing their anger, who accused God of reneging on His promises, who felt abandoned. If the sacred writers could address the Almighty in such a frank, unmitigated way, then I could too. I began railing at God.

You promised to be with us always. Where were You when I was so young and felt so alone? I was so little! So small. Where were you? How about when Chuck was on top of me? I was naive, didn't know what was happening. Then all those boys who used me. I felt so trapped! I didn't know how to stop them. Why didn't you protect me? Stop them? Show me a way out? I needed you! Where were you?

At one point I didn't know if I was talking to my Heavenly Father or my earthly one. It didn't matter. I let nothing stop me, not even a critical mind that tried to accuse me of having a pity party, of putting on a show. I let out all my grievances, then went on to list others sufferings. Until nothing was left.

At first, my words seemed to fly off into vacant space. But then I began to sense some kind of listening presence in the room. In the end I knew – more than I did not know – that God had been there, that unlike my parents, my anger had not sent Him away. He had not buckled over.

He had stayed with me, patiently listening, and would do so for as long as it took. And that meant everything.

I wasn't sure I wanted to remain in my profession. What I wanted most of all was to help others know that God is present and will meet their deepest needs and desires. Working within a church seemed the natural way to go. I asked my pastor if our church would consider hiring a lay person. With my counseling background I could visit the sick and homebound, counsel those struggling with various life situations and teach and facilitate spiritual growth groups. He told me that our church could not financially add any additional staff. Yet this did not diminish my desire.

What I needed was legitimacy, the right credentials, a different degree. Could I do this in my mid-fifties with limited financial resources? It was either this, taking another low paying job, or going back to a profession that didn't seem to want me. I decided to apply to seminary and then see what would happen.

The application process proved a bit daunting. First, I needed references from a pastor, a lay leader and a work colleague or friend. Asking for these felt like I was imposing. Yet, all three readily agreed and checked *excellent* or *very good* on all the listed personal/spiritual qualities and interpersonal relationships.

In response to a question about my weaknesses, a work colleague wrote, "Eileen's passion about an issue can sometimes stand in the way of practicality." At first I was a bit offended by this criticism but then thought, *How did she know that? She really nailed it! And said it with such understatement. My passion has stood in the way, not only of practicality but of sanity!*

In May of 2001, I was accepted as a part-time student in the Master of Arts in Theological Studies program. In August, I stepped into my first class. Carrying a book bag with three sharpened pencils, two pens, a thin lined spiral notebook and two required Church History textbooks, I quickly took a seat in the back and watched students younger than my sons file in.

Seminary study imparted much more than knowledge. It brought understanding and healing of the misconceptions that had surrounded my time with Sarah. It gave explanations other than being crazy, immoral or demon-possessed for my behavior.

I learned that scripture can be approached in different ways. Literalists like Beverly generally believed that God had conveyed His Word into the minds of scribes, who wrote it down. All scripture was the inspired word of God, without error. "God said it, I believe it, that settles it" was their mantra.

Scholars also took the Bible seriously, but not literally. They viewed scripture as written by men, inspired to make sense of their encounters with God. The writers, with their various voices and perspectives, lived in different times and cultures from ours. Thus, in order to arrive at the meaning of a particular passage, we must be aware of it's cultural and historical context.

As hermeneutics gave me a greater appreciation of human beings role in the writing of scripture, a class on spiritual direction gave me a greater appreciation of God's role in the writing of my life.

Our first assignment was to write a six page autobiography about how the scriptures, the church, other Christians and the Holy Spirit have guided you. This felt daunting. I didn't think I had enough to fill six pages, especially since scripture had misguided me and the church had let me down. Yet, having to meet the requirement, I began writing about my earliest years:

> It was primarily through nature that I experienced a sense of well-being, belonging and security. As a young child I felt protected, watched over, by the two tall pine trees which grew on either side of our house. As a school-aged child living in the country, I spent much of my time outdoors. It was here that I felt uninhibited and could breathe deeply. This was "church" to me. . . in nature I experienced life and felt nurtured. Even while in the Lutheran church my family attended, it was the trees just

outside the glass partition at the front of the altar that I was most attracted to.

My early church experiences were also significant, although I have not always recognized this. It was sitting in the church pew week after week with my family that I experienced a sense of belonging I felt nowhere else. I was intrigued by the enthusiasm of the Sunday school superintendent who kept showing up year after year. I drank in the positive affirmations and patient instruction of the junior choir director.

I wrote about people who had influenced me as an adult: Pastor Vic, who I teamed with to make evangelism calls, who listened and never got to the questions we were supposed to ask. Beverly and our little bible study group. My friendship with Linda. I wrote about coming out of deception by confessing all I had done to friends. I wrote about the lay school and the silent prayer retreat.

The final part of the assignment was to cite the means that I had used to grow in Christian understanding and experience. My list included prayer, Bible meditation, journal writing, contact with nature, worship, small group interaction and spiritual direction. I doubted whether I'd keep all this up, yet thought my list was pretty impressive.

The instructor did not see it this way. At the bottom of the page she wrote, "And what do you do to play? This, too, is God – Blessings on the journey." *What?! That's all you have to say? After all I'm doing you bring up my need to play? That's it? Nothing about how hard I'm trying? PLAY? That's what God wants from me?*

Lectures that defined aspects of the spiritual life gave me a broader, more accepting understanding of Christianity and of my own journey. Von Hugel cited three phases of holistic spiritual development: the Institutional (traditional), the Critical (reasoning) and the Mystical (inner world). All are needed. I could use a bit more of the reasoning kind.

In the book, *The Critical Journey*, J.O. Hagberg and R.A. Guelich describe six stages in the life of faith: Stage one is the recognition of God, or a spiritual awakening. Stage two is being involved in a group or church where there is often a sense of "I've found IT." For me, I had found the one, right way with Beverly. Stage three is the productive life where one engages in ministry, uses one's gifts and takes risks.

Stage four is the journey inward, a place of suffering and uncertainty, of hitting the wall. As an essential part of our journey, it is where we face our residual mistrust of God and our own ego and where we deal with the mystery of God. This was an amazingly accurate description of my interior angst after Sarah. But what was even more amazing, and affirming, was that going through this stage is an essential part of our journey.

Stage five, the journey outward, is where one experiences a deeper encounter with grace and trust in God, where a relationship of non-contingency begins. God doesn't love me *because* . . . He just loves me. And finally, stage six, the life of love, is where one is not concerned with position or prestige. With less focus on self and the need for affirmation, one is free to cultivate a deeper compassion for others.

After two semesters I decided not to pursue a degree. Being able to manage only two classes at a time, I knew it would take years to complete a degree and by then I'd be close to sixty. The prospect of any church hiring me over someone much younger was unlikely.

Although there would be no career change, I was not yet ready to return to my old one, so I audited some classes in Marriage and Family Studies.

A lecture around the need for integration pointed out that God has given us two avenues of truth He wants us to know. One is general revelation found in psychology, science, art, literature and nature. The other is special revelation found in the scriptures. This left me breathless. A revered professor from a Christian institution of higher learning said that truth can be known, not only through the scriptures, but through human culture.

The lecture continued. Both theology and the social sciences are human endeavors. Neither is more worthwhile, yet there is bad science and bad theology (how well I knew). Since good theology and good science are not contradictory, our job is to unite them, not to absorb one into the other. In this integration process each discipline retains its own identity while benefiting from the other's perspective and communicating the same truth.

Suddenly I understood the mistake I'd made with Sarah. Clinging to the fundamentalist belief that the Bible and God was all that was needed, I dismissed psychology's perspective. I did not acknowledge its legitimate role of assessing and treating persons (not saints) suffering from mental disorders.

A teaching about self-differentiation (the definition of self within relationships) belatedly defined what I lacked with Sarah. Differentiation is the ability to care deeply in a controlled way, to maintain both individuality and connection, to value self and be authentic. Differentiation allows the therapist to choose, not to react. So, above all else, the therapist must notice and manage her own feelings and anxiety around client issues. The sense of fixing or running away can be a sign of undifferentiation.

Other classes reviewed things I'd already been taught. Feeling more competent and running out of money (I had been living off the sale of my portion of the land David, Pam and I had inherited from our parents) I knew I must return to my profession. A classmate told me of a Christian mental health clinic south of Eau Claire. I met with two women and was offered a psychotherapist contract position.

Chapter Twenty-Two

I was excited. The position gave me the independence of being on my own, under no one's supervision, yet without the pressure of marketing myself or managing a business. Clients would be given to me out of the pool of new referrals and a percentage of my pay would go toward clinic expenses.

I was responsible for furnishing my office (I bought three used upholstered chairs, a lamp and some pictures and a colleague loaned me her old desk and swivel chair). I would also need to purchase malpractice insurance, fill out credentialing insurance forms, and hire a tax consultant.

Early on I was asked by Helen, the director, if I'd like to take a client with a bi-polar diagnosis and a history of hospitalizations as this would be a long term, stable source of income. I thanked her for the offer but said I'd prefer not to take this type of client as my focus was on brief, solution-focused therapy. What I did not mention, however, was my fear of suffocating under the weight of another overly dependent person.

I was not offered another long-term client. This suited me just fine. It seemed to suit the clinic also. Others schedules were often filled with long-term clients, whereas I was always open to take new referrals, often those seeking counseling for the first time.

Within a short time I learned to manage my caseload in a way that suited me. Seeing a new client each hour left me feeling rushed so I left fifteen or thirty minutes between appointments. Scheduling seven clients a day left my head spinning so I limited it to five. All these decisions meant less income, but that was not a priority. What I most wanted was to be fully present to the client and to whatever was going on in me, to create a space where clients could freely express themselves. This was not always easy.

Mel, a hard working physical laborer in his mid-fifties, believed people should do the right thing, follow the rules. He was particularly offended by a neighbor who violated private property ordinances. Mel repeatedly took this to the city council but got no results. He had recently been kicked out of the meetings for being disruptive and going beyond his allotted time. This made him even more livid. To appease his wife, Mel agreed to see a counselor.

During our third session I wanted to kick him out. After patiently listening, after expressing empathy and offering alternative ways of perceiving and acting, I was done. But he wasn't. So I gently placed my hands on the arms of the chair, settled into the seat, breathed, listened some more, and finally heard.

Beneath Mel's obnoxious behavior was a man with a passion for justice, for righting wrongs. I felt empathy toward him and told him how difficult it must be to see so much in the world that was wrong and not be able to do anything about it. Since he did not return I'm not sure this did any good, whether he changed. But I know I did. A power beyond me (some would call it grace) had gifted me with a liberating sense of compassion.

I suppose I started feeling too secure in my autonomy, too comfortable with the friendly colleague whose office was kitty corner to mine. We began having conversations about our work. I knew I was going out on a limb, but my need to find the truth was greater than my fear, so I began posing questions that had been banging around in my head since working in a mental hospital.

I wondered whether the medical model, with its scientific, biological approach to illness, was the best template for treating mental disorders. Couldn't its focus on the individual neglect where the real problem might lie – within the family? or community? Couldn't a diagnosis become a person's identity, leading to dependency on an outside expert? Might this stop the person from taking responsibility for his own life?

Greg patiently listened, then calmly explained that some clients need one stable, consistent long-term relationship in their lives, that they do progress, but only by taking very small steps, often around abusive, toxic family members. I thanked him for explaining this so clearly and finally felt an openness and appreciation for long-term professional treatment.

A few weeks later Helen called me into her office to discuss "some serious matters." A woman I had seen two months ago had complained about my lack of empathy around her son. I immediately recalled who she was. I had assessed her as co-dependent and had tried to address this, very directly. "You can't keep taking your son in whenever he messes up. This is not helping him. He has to learn the consequences of his actions so he can become responsible for himself. He needs to find another place to live. He's an adult, he'll find a way, he's done it before. Give him a move-out date, then stick to it."

I wasn't surprised that the client had had strong objections to this, so strong that she was mulling it over two months later. I too had experienced an urgent need to help another and knew how insidious it could become, how hard it was to recognize and change a way of being that seemed so right – that gave your life meaning and worth.

I tried to defend myself to Helen. I said that out of all the clients I'd seen, only one had voiced a complaint, and rather reluctantly, two months later. I offered to see the client again, to apologize. No, that would not be needed; they had taken care of it.

Helen then brought up my refusal to accept long-term clients. I retorted that I thought I had been clear that my expertise was in providing short-term, solution-focused therapy. She continued. Greg had been offended by our recent conversation. Finally, recognizing that the case had been made and I could do nothing, I thought, *I've been here before. Why can't I learn to keep my mouth shut?*

Just before leaving, a newly hired therapist told me of a Christian clinic that was opening a new branch in the northern suburbs, closer to my home. I immediately called and a job interview was set up.

It felt reassuring to talk with three men, one who was an ordained minister with a doctorate in psychology. Other than skipping over the fact of being fired from my last job, I spoke as straightforward as they had. When I finished they did not ask for job references as I feared. They offered me a job.

After a tour of their beautiful new facility, I was asked if I'd like to select some decorative pictures and accessories for my office. Of course they would pay, just turn in the receipts. Already feeling like a trusted and valued colleague, I immediately set upon the task. I was delighted to find reasonably priced, handsome pieces. As I stood in the middle of my spacious, well-lit, second story office (my previous one was small, with one ground level window), unbounded gratitude welled up. Once more I had been given a fresh start.

Although gaining clients was a slow process and the pay was less, it soon became apparent that this was a more suitable workplace for me. Most of the clinicians were trained in marriage and family therapy, a solution-focused discipline in sync with my own orientation. A computer program that formulated treatment plans to fit particular diagnoses made record keeping a snap, even enjoyable. There were places to socialize and I quickly formed a lighthearted relationship with Jane, the receptionist.

Marriage counseling became my greatest challenge. My only formal education had been the few classes I took at seminary. And since my own marriage had failed, I questioned whether I had the right to counsel others.

Feeling ill prepared, I searched for anything that might help. I gathered articles: The Five Secrets of Effective Communication, Ten Attitudes that Keep You from Expressing your Feelings, A Proven Five-Step Approach to Managing Conflict, Five Relationship Myths, and so on. I attended workshops on Addressing Common Dilemmas in Couples Therapy and Understanding and Treating Infidelity.

I cut out a cartoon of a dog and cat lying next to each other in bed with the caption, *Exasperated? Try to Think of Your Mate as a Cross-Cultural Experience!* and showed it to couples who might benefit from a little humor.

I offered whatever I could. Nothing seemed to work. Most couples came after years of conflict and silent discord. Often one party had already bailed out of the marriage while the other was desperately trying to save it. Listening to a history of grievances, of blaming and defending, was painful. Trying to teach better ways of communicating when one party triggered habitual, defensive reactions in the other seemed fruitless.

I began to question whether setting up a time for couples to talk about their relationship did more harm than good. I worried about what happened between the couple after they walked out of the office. An experienced counselor said that often the best we could do was help couples work out amicable ways to separate or divorce. This recognition of our limitations brought some peace.

One seemingly helpful method was to help couples focus, not on their argument or discord, but on the repair work that happened afterwards – on the simple, private gesture or action that bridged the disconnect

One couple showed that, with tenacity, over time a marriage could be saved. Mike had cheated on Shirley. The most destructive part was not the affair but all the lies. Mike agreed to disclose anything Shirley needed to know. Shirley felt insecure about his whereabouts so Mike checked in with her throughout the day, came home on time, called if he was going to be late. Mike bought her flowers, took her to nice restaurants, planned romantic get-aways. Shirley cried. As they began to envision a future together, I knew they had turned the corner of a difficult, painful journey.

A sure way to evaluate whether our practice was getting off track was to ask if we were working harder than the client. In marriage counseling I was definitely working harder than anyone else. It was exhausting, but more than that, it was discouraging. I asked not to be assigned any more couples, *just for a while*. I never resumed marriage counseling. Over the next year my caseload decreased considerably, which contributed to my decision to retire.

When I turned sixty-two and became illegible for social security, I waited six more months, just to make sure, before retiring.

As I look back now, what stands out is the privilege of being let into the lives of so many people. My profession increased my capacity to accept even the most difficult person, and in the process to become more accepting and compassionate toward myself. Getting to know people from different classes, cultures and lifestyles broadened by mind and enriched my life.

My profession kept me mindful of the need for God's grace and guidance. On the drive home I often felt satisfied and exhausted. I had finished the day's work, given what I could, stayed true to my self, at least done no harm. I would probably never know whether or how I helped. But God knew. Any good that remained was His doing. I prayed that everything else would fall away.

Chapter Twenty-Three

Retirement brought a new sense of freedom. Freedom to try new things, to grow, to reinvent myself. Given my propensity toward solitude, and no job that required me to interact with others, I knew I could become too isolated so I decided to talk with people wherever I went. I was amazed at how delightful simple conversation, with no purpose other than finding something in common, could be.

To help these conversations along I consciously brought skills developed through my profession. Skills like being curious, listening well and asking a few questions before relaying whatever I had to say. And I had a lot to say. Sometimes I talked until the person's eyes began to glaze over.

I also delighted to find ways – any way – of connecting with my five grandchildren. Recently I competed in a burping contest with brothers Aryan, twelve, and Jeremy, ten (I won), took photos of flowers with artistic thirteen-year-old Madison, mimicked a sign language only five-year-old Olivia and I understood, and allowed sixteen-year-old Bret to drive my new SUV while I sat next to him, breathing. As I see all the different personalities and interests that continue to emerge, I wonder what kind of career they will chose and who their life partners will be. If they ever get in a jam, I hope I can be someone they can turn to.

Paul and I were able to engage in pleasant, casual conversation during the kids' events and family holidays. He died of alcoholism three years ago and I treasure the time we spent together while he was in hospice.

My sister-in-law and I have become good friends. Mia lives in Virginia, so we don't see each other often, but when we do, we immediately relate as if no time has passed. I find her candidness refreshing (and sometimes irritating). We have also become good traveling companions and have taken Road Scholar (previously Elderhostel) trips together. We lived for a week in a cabin near Eagle Lake. After David died, we returned to scatter his ashes over the water.

In retirement interest groups became a ready-made way to meet people. Each time I ventured into one, I felt that same high school trepidation. *Will I fit in? Be accepted? Be competent?*

I took a number of senior enrichment classes at a local university. I felt exhilarated as I walked the six blocks to campus and even more so when I discovered how much I enjoyed taking classes outside of psychology and theology. Once again the greater world had opened it's arms to me.

I joined a bi-monthly writers group. At first, listening and critiquing a twenty-minute read was daunting. Receiving their critiques was somewhere between unnerving and terrifying. I am now so grateful for all their suggestions and encouragement. They kept me writing when I felt like giving up.

I joined a book club and found that as a writer I became a better reader. My contributions have been warmly received, yet I realize I can dominate the discussion so I try to curb my enthusiasm (well, mostly) by sitting back and waiting for others to speak.

At the YMCA, instead of my usual solitary activities – swimming laps, biking or walking on the treadmill – I decided to try some groups. After finding Pilates too hard and yoga too soft, I looked into a senior fitness class. When I saw them sitting down on chairs I walked away. *Surely this is not where I belong!* I am now a regular member and bask in being in the middle of a gym filled with older women (and maybe a dozen men), moving in synch to rocking music.

Painting classes have not been so rewarding. Feeling anxious and inept, I often sped ahead, putting something – anything – on the canvas before I froze. Nothing I did was remotely painterly. If I happened to glance at another's piece, my self-esteem plummeted even more.

At home, alone, unwilling to accept failure, I often reworked the painting. Most of the time I was, if not delighted, at least satisfied with the finished work. Perhaps the feeling I had when I first put a canvas, tubes of paint and a jar of brushes on my newspaper-lined table was true: *This is me! This is where I belong. Inside an artist is just waiting to be set free.*

I left the anonymity of a mega church and joined a smaller congregation. Every week I ventured out of my comfort zone and engaged in conversation with someone I did not yet know. Attending a women's weekend retreat accelerated this process.

Knowing I could always find reasons not to volunteer, I determined to do whatever was asked of me. I wrote a few brochures and newspaper articles, took part in planning adult education, facilitated seminary lay classes, led a writer's group, served coffee.

My greatest struggle was being in a women's Bible study. I bristled at interpretations that saw us as the favored, chosen ones (always by grace) who were superior (yet spoken with a tone of humility) to those outside the faith. This was too familiar, too close. Thinking that I must confront it, my tone became too intense, my words, abrasive. This was not the way to make friends. I tried to change by talking more softly, by remaining silent, yet nothing stopped the inner turmoil and my need to speak out. I stopped going after a year.

I left this church, twice, to join larger churches that offered more diversified and scholarly classes. I came back, twice, because I missed a sense of community. Many have told me they're glad I'm back. I'm starting to believe them.

Perhaps I'll stay this time. But I'm not sure. Leaving is a life-long pattern. I leave situations and relationships when I feel unwanted or oppressed. I leave to create emotional space, to connect with my in-depth self, to begin anew.

I pull out my box of greeting cards and find the one I bought some years ago. On the front of the card a woman pledges, "I am not codependent! I Swear I'm not!" Inside she continues, "I'm simply a concerned, loving, caring, totally unselfish, selfless, self-denying, self-sacrificing human being, who gives to the point of complete self-destruction."

Of course this is meant to be humorous, yet I do not laugh. It comes way too close to describing me. My codependence, taken in as a child and spurred on by occupational values and religious beliefs, became so much a part of my identity and sense of worth that, until I took it to its natural conclusion, I could not see it for what it was. Only then could I begin to change.

Standing in front of my dresser, I notice some of the things that remind me of who I am. The November angel I bought when I was a clerk at Penney's is still there, along with a figurine of a little girl with closed eyes, nestled into the palm of a large hand. A small photo of a young, radiant woman with a natural, gentle smile, stylish hair and smooth skin is propped in front of a simply crafted wood jewelry box. It was taken just after I divorced and reminds me that the beautiful woman in the photo still resides in me.

A yellow toy kayak, a miniature version of the one I bought after I moved into a small house by a lake, is next to the jewelry box. I've paddled beside racing sailboats, red-eyed loons, schools of carp, and diving turtles. I've taken pictures of sailboats at sunset, soaring seagulls, acrobatic kite surfers and elaborate sandcastles.

This lake, like Eagle Lake, has become a life-giving sanctuary. Whenever I walk to the shore I feel my breath deepen and relax. As I sit on the bench at the end of the dock, gazing at the unbroken expanse of water, I am engulfed with a sense of freedom and safety and feel a deep sense of gratitude for a way of life that I thought would end by now.

A small photo sits on either side of my November angel. One is of Dad and me standing unusually close. Dad is wearing his Rauma cap and although he is not smiling, neither is he frowning. I am smiling. My arm rests on top of an open car door, like I am about to leave. What I am most drawn to is the golden, overexposed light that surrounds us.

The other photo is taken just outside my parents' home. Pam and I stand in the back, Mom and Grandma are staggered in front of us. We all smile warmly. One of my hands is around Mom's waist and the other on Gramma's arm. I remember asking for the picture to be taken "to have one of just the women."

A drawing of a little girl, maybe three or four, hangs on the wall above the dresser. It was cropped from a larger picture of Jesus surrounded by children of different colors and races. The girl's dark eyes gaze up, imploringly. Her hands, palms together, fingers stretched out, are held in front of her, beholding, beseeching the one she gazes upon.

One of my photo greeting cards hangs next to the drawing. The sun is sinking beneath the horizon. Its golden, orange hue is reflected in calm waters bordered by wispy reeds and a simple dock. Underneath the photo are the words, *With each new day comes an opportunity for a new beginning.*

Being seventy-two means taking care of the aches and disorders that inevitably come. Benign vertigo is one of mine. During a particularly rough time, to help my balance, I received treatment by a physical therapist. In one of our sessions Heidi directed me to close my eyes, turn my head back and forth, stand on one foot. I knew I might fall and expressed reluctance.

Heidi moved behind me, stretched out her arms, and softly said, "It's alright, I've gotcha." Although her words were common, they sounded like nothing I had ever heard before yet had always known to be true. God's word, relieving my hidden fear, giving me the only thing I need to know. *It's alright. I've gotcha. No matter what happens, I've gotcha.*